"Read this book! But only if you are looking for the perfect road map to get through your MFT education and licensing process with the least amount of stress and the most amount of fun possible. It is a treasure of a handbook."
~ Casey Truffo, MFT, coach, speaker, and author of Be A Wealthy Therapist: Finally You Can Make A Living While Making A Difference

"This is the first book I recommend to pre-licensed MFTs to get through the licensing process with confidence and ease."
~ Milena Esherick, PsyD, M.A. in Counseling Psychology Program Director, The Wright Institute

"This book helps prepare pre-licensed and licensed Marriage and Family Therapists for the steps from graduate school to opening a successful private practice. I highly recommend this book!"
~ Dr. Charles Billings, PhD, FAClinP, FAFamP, MFT, Department Chair, Counseling Psychology, Dominican University of California

"This author offers great insight into the experience and unique challenges of becoming a licensed Marriage and Family Therapist."
~ Angela Lamson, PhD, LMFT, CFLE, Family Therapy Program Director and Associate Professor, East Carolina University

"Whether you are an MFT Trainee, Intern, or already have your license, I highly recommend getting this book. It offers a lot of practical advice and ideas to help you navigate through the process, make better decisions, and be better prepared each step along the way. I wish it had been available when I was getting started."
~ Howard Spector, President and Owner, www.TrackYourHours.com

"Cris Walker Roskelley's handbook for newly-minted MFTs will help them get oriented and determine their professional path after graduate school. Her book helps pre-licensed and licensed MFTs get through the licensing process, stay motivated, and move forward into a successful practice."
~ Lynn Grodzki, LCSW, MCC, Private Practice Success

On the Road
To Becoming A *Successful*
Marriage and Family Therapist

An Insider's Handbook
From Graduate School Through Licensure...
and Beyond!

Cris Walker Roskelley, MFT

ON THE ROAD TO BECOMING A SUCCESSFUL MARRIAGE AND FAMILY THERAPIST: An Insider's Handbook from Graduate School Through Licensure... and Beyond! by Cris Walker Roskelley

Published by:
Femme Osage Publishing
St. Louis, MO 63376
www.BusinessBuildingBooks.com

Copyright © 2008 Cris Walker Roskelley
Printed in the United States of America

ISBN: 978-1-934509-20-3

Library of Congress Control Number: 2008934436

Special permission for excerpts granted by:

Copyright © 2002 by Irvin D. Yalom
Reprinted by permission of HarperCollins Publishers

Copyright © 2003 by Jeffrey A. Kottler
Reprinted by permission of John Wiley & Sons, Inc.

Copyright © 2003 by Lynn Grodzki
Reprinted by permission of author

Copyright © 2003 by Mary Pipher
Reprinted by permission of author

This book is available at special discounts for bulk purchases for educational institutions.

Preface

This is an exciting time in the psychotherapy field. With the continued growth of the internet, the practice of therapy continues to grow and evolve... for the better! In the following pages, you will encounter stories of my own experiences as well as many tips, both my own and from other MFT professionals, for navigating the road ahead. I have also included quotations from leading experts in the field of psychotherapy.

There is not enough room in one book to include everything you need to know about being a Marriage and Family Therapist. I have referenced several additional resources you may want to explore. A comprehensive listing of these resources can be found in Appendices E and F.

Be sure to visit the links section of my website for exclusive discounts to many products including exam study materials, marketing resources, practice management solutions, CEUs, and more.

Wishing you a successful MFT journey,

Cris Walker Roskelley, MFT
www.MFTHandbook.com

Acknowledgements

To thank everyone who supported the development of this book would be nearly impossible as the information in this book came from my own MFT journey, to which so many contributed.

Among those that stand out are each member of the ever-expanding Walker clan, Stacy Mann, Cathy Nabbefeld, Grinnell Morris, Dianne Kraaijvanger, Melyssa Nelson, Tamara Hostetler, Dr. Charles Billings, Ginia Laudisio, Mary Riemersma, Rachel Byrne, Sherry Whyte, Susan Peters, Wendy Kirk, Dr. Daniel and Hannah Gottsegen, Wendy Heffner, Tracey Gersten, Nancy Hawkins, Lynne and Larry Klippel at Femme Osage Publishing, Casey Truffo, Lynn Grodzki, Mary and Jim Pipher, Jeffrey Kottler, Irvin Yalom, and Daniel Minuchin.

Special thanks to my husband for editing and support, and to my faithful and beloved beagle, who patiently sat with (or slept next to) me during every hour of this book's creation.

I sincerely thank everyone mentioned here, and those I may have overlooked, for their guidance, friendship, and assistance in making this book a reality.

Warning - Disclaimer

The information presented in this book is intended to help you navigate the lengthy and often confusing road to licensure as a Marriage and Family Therapist. It is sold with the understanding that the author is not engaged in rendering legal, accounting, or other professional services. While there are specific suggestions and tips included in this book, every person must make their own decisions and choices as to their unique path to licensure. The author assumes no liability or responsibility to any person or entity with respect to any loss or damage caused, or alleged to have been caused, directly or indirectly, by the information, suggestions, and/or tips contained in this book.

For Lee – the road to my heart

Contents

SECTION ONE:
The Therapy Three

Chapter 1
Introduction

Congratulations! You now have an insider's survival guide to navigating the many twists and turns along the road to becoming a licensed and successful Marriage and Family Therapist (MFT).

Do any of the following questions apply to you?

- Are you thinking about becoming an MFT?

- Are you currently enrolled in an MFT graduate program?

- Have you graduated from an MFT graduate program and are working toward licensure?

- Are you a recently licensed MFT?

- Are you in private practice as an MFT?

If you answered yes to any of the above, then this book is for you!

How Will This Book Help Me?

There are three stages to becoming a licensed and successful MFT. I like to call these "The Therapy Three":

1. Graduate School
2. Getting the Hours
3. Passing the Exams

On the Road to Becoming a Successful Marriage and Family Therapist: An Insider's Handbook from Graduate School Through Licensure... and Beyond! offers one-stop shopping to demystify The Therapy Three, helping you navigate the tricky road toward becoming a successful and licensed MFT in private practice. This is not a textbook. This is a hands-on, been-through-it road map on how to survive the long road ahead and make it to the finish line... becoming a licensed and successful MFT!

You now have a road map for success. There are hard-earned tips to make the journey a lot less stressful and to keep you from losing your focus and motivation. Confusing state board requirements are explained in straightforward language. Common assumptions are clarified, and mistakes are flagged so you can best avoid them. Suggestions for reflection and introspection help you get what you need from The Therapy Three to reach your MFT goals.

My hope for you is that, after reading this book, you will be informed of exactly what the MFT road entails and be able to answer the following questions:

- Do I want to be an MFT?

- How long will it take?

- What are the insider tricks to make the process easier or faster?

- What do I want to do with my license?

- How do I strike a balance between the personal and professional while becoming and being an MFT?

- Once I'm licensed, then what?

The helping profession consists of individuals with various mental health licenses, including but not limited to the Licensed Marriage and Family Therapist (MFT), Licensed Clinical Social Worker (LCSW), the Psychologist (PhD and PsyD), and the Licensed Professional Counselor (LPC). This book focuses on the Master's level Licensed Marriage and Family Therapist (MFT).

While examples and terminology in this book use California as the licensing state, the material and strategies included will be relevant to anyone on the MFT road.

How Should I Use This Book?

Whether you are pre-licensed, licensed, or just thinking about becoming a Marriage and Family Therapist, I encourage you to read this book initially in its entirety. This approach will give you a useful bird's eye view of the road ahead.

It will then be a good idea to re-read each section depending on where you are in the process to ensure that you are making the best choices for yourself at every turn along the MFT road.

> *"Whatever you can do, or dream you can, begin it. Boldness has genius, power and magic in it."*
> ~ W. H. Murray

Chapter 2
The Therapy Three

The practice of Marriage and Family Therapy is rewarding, fulfilling, and deeply moving. The path of getting licensed, on the other hand, can be confusing, depleting, and frustrating. It doesn't need to be this way!

Having a thorough understanding of what is ahead of you will enable you to make the best choices for yourself from the beginning. Your journey toward licensure and the establishment of a successful private practice can be an exciting, productive, and growth-oriented experience.

As mentioned in the introduction, there are three stages to becoming a licensed and successful MFT that I like to call "The Therapy Three":

1. Graduate School
2. Getting the Hours
3. Passing the Exams

Detailed information and insider tips on navigating each stage of The Therapy Three will be explored throughout this book to ensure you are prepared and ready to reach your goals of becoming a licensed and successful MFT.

Many start or are already on the road to becoming an MFT without truly understanding what is ahead of them. Some get midway through graduate school (or farther!) before realizing it is not the right road for them or that it was much longer than they had anticipated.

Anyone considering or pursuing the MFT path should be more informed of the intricacies of the licensure process and, yet, shockingly few are. Why?

Those considering a career in Marriage and Family Therapy often ask licensed MFTs about their experience within the profession but may not ask about the actual licensing process. Therefore, many do not receive the nuts and bolts of what is entailed on the road to becoming an MFT.

Those who do inquire about the licensing process often do not get the straight scoop. Perhaps newly licensed MFTs are so exhausted from their own journey that they are just excited to put the licensing experience behind them and focus on the next stage of their career.

If asked about the path to licensure, some MFTs may often forget the details of their experience (or have blocked them out!) so that those thinking about starting their own journey do not get the full picture of what is ahead.

As in many professions, there also seems to be an unspoken "pay your dues" mentality: I suffered, so why shouldn't you? The grueling path toward licensure is often seen as a rite of passage into the field.

For example, most MFT-hopefuls do not know and are not told that the majority of "Getting the Hours" are often *unpaid*. I researched the MFT field in depth before pursuing it and never heard anything about working for free. Similar to most of my graduate school classmates, I thought that the post-graduate clinical work would be similar to that of a medical doctor's (M.D.), where a doctor is paid through residency. Not always so!

On the Road to Becoming a Successful Licensed Marriage and Family Therapist: An Insider's Handbook from Graduate School Through Licensure... and Beyond! unveils such surprises and offers tips to help you succeed. You will learn the secrets to navigating each stage of The Therapy Three en route to MFT licensure and forward into private practice to make the process faster, easier, and more rewarding.

"Success always comes when preparation meets opportunity."

~ Henry Hartman

Chapter 3
The MFT Profession

In the United States, the profession of Marriage and Family Therapy is regulated at the state level. At the time of this writing, 48 states plus the District of Columbia currently recognize and license Marriage and Family Therapists. West Virginia and Montana are the only two states that have not yet passed legislation to license Marriage and Family Therapists.

Marriage and Family Therapy

The American Association for Marriage and Family Therapy (AAMFT) is the national professional association for Marriage and Family Therapists in the United States. There are also state MFT associations. All of these associations represent and promote the professional interests of MFTs.

Following are excerpts from the AAMFT's consumer brochure titled "A Career for the Future: Marriage and Family Therapy."

What is Marriage and Family Therapy?

In marriage and family therapy, the unit of treatment isn't just the person - even if only a single person is interviewed - it is the set of relationships in which the person is imbedded. A family's patterns of behavior influence the individual and, therefore, may need to be a part of the treatment plan.

Marriage and family therapists treat a wide range of serious clinical problems including: depression, marital problems, anxiety, individual psychological problems, and child-parent problems.

Research indicates that marriage and family therapy is as effective, and in some cases more effective than standard and/or individual treatments for many mental health problems such as: adult schizophrenia, affective (mood) disorders, adult alcoholism and drug abuse, children's conduct disorders, adolescent drug abuse, anorexia in young adult women, childhood autism, chronic physical illness in adults and children, and marital distress and conflict.

Who are Marriage and Family Therapists?

MFTs are specialists in relationships and treat persons who are involved in interpersonal relationships. Marriage and Family Therapists are mental health professionals who are trained in psychotherapy and family systems, and are licensed to diagnose and treat mental and emotional disorders within the context of marriage, couples and family systems.

MFTs are a highly experienced group of practitioners. They evaluate and treat mental and emotional disorders, other health and behavioral problems, and address a wide array of relationship issues within the context of the family system.

MFTs broaden the traditional emphasis on the individual to attend

> to the nature and role of individuals in primary relationship networks such as marriage and the family. MFTs take a holistic perspective to health care; they are concerned with the overall, long-term well being of individuals and their families.
>
> MFTs have graduate training (a Master's or Doctoral degree) in marriage and family therapy and at least two years of clinical experience. Marriage and family therapists are recognized as a "core" mental health profession, along with psychiatry, psychology, social work and psychiatric nursing. Since 1970 there has been a 50-fold increase in the number of marriage and family therapists. At any given time they are treating over 1.8 million people.[1]

The California Association of Marriage and Family Therapists (CAMFT) adds:

> [MFTs] are trained to assess, diagnose and treat individuals, couples, families and groups to achieve more adequate, satisfying

---

1   American Association for Marriage and Family Therapy. *A Career for the Future: Marriage and Family Therapy* [Brochure]. AAMFT: Author.

> and productive marriage, family and social adjustment. The practice also includes premarital counseling, child counseling, divorce or separation counseling and other relationship counseling.[2]

The average MFT goes through three years of full-time graduate school, followed by at least two years (and often many more) of "getting the hours" in post-graduate clinical internships before studying for and taking the licensing exam(s).

Today, more than 50,000 Marriage and Family Therapists treat individuals, couples, and families nationwide. California alone currently has 82 MFT graduate programs.

---

2   California Association of Marriage and Family Therapists. *"What is an MFT?"* <www.camft.org>.

Chapter 4
You're On Your Way

Perhaps the MFT path attracted you as a result of your own family of origin issues. Maybe your interest comes purely from an altruistic place. Yet again, maybe this route seems like a good fit due to the financial allure or freedom of being your own boss.

Take a moment to think about why you are interested in embarking on this road or why you have already begun the journey.

Maintaining awareness of your intentions and motivations will help sustain you during the long road ahead.

> *"Much of the early therapy training that many of us received occurred growing up in our own families, where we acted as go-betweens, conflict mediators, and helpers."*
> *~ Jeffrey A. Kottler,*
> On Being a Therapist

I want to become an MFT because:

_____

_____

_____

My role in my family was:

_____

_____

_____

Being a therapist will help me to:

_____

_____

_____

Whatever your motivation, it is important to truly understand what is required on the road to becoming a successful licensed Marriage and Family Therapist. Only when you truly know what is required, will you be able to make an informed decision about what you want and how best to get there.

SECTION TWO:
Graduate School

Chapter 5
Choosing the Best Graduate School

There are several criteria to consider in choosing an MFT graduate program. To determine the best program for yourself, think about the following factors and their priority of importance to you and any others affected by your program choice.

Accreditation

Be aware that there are different levels of accreditation for MFT graduate schools. Accreditation simply means a process by which the quality of a program is established and maintained. Most of you will be attending either an "approved" or an "accredited" MFT degree program.

In California, "accredited" means that a graduate program has been accredited by the Western Association of Schools and Colleges

(WASC). "Approved" means that a graduate program has been approved by the Bureau of Private Post-Secondary Education.

A significant benefit to graduating from an accredited school is that your degree will usually be recognized by other state licensing boards. This consideration is important if you foresee that you might move or wish to become licensed in a different state than where your graduate program is located.

Note: The American Association for Marriage and Family Therapy (AAMFT) has its own accrediting body called the Commission on Accreditation for Marriage and Family Therapy Education (COAMFTE).

While a school that is accredited by COAMFTE meets a rigorous set of academic standards, it is certainly possible to receive an equally strong education at a program that is not COAMFTE-accredited.

What is most important is finding the best graduate school for you. There are many factors to consider in your preparation to becoming a Marriage and Family Therapist, and accreditation is only one ingredient.

Program Quality

Not all MFT programs are made equal. It is ultimately possible to become a licensed MFT by attending most any MFT program. However, it is important to attend a program that will prepare you not only to pass the state licensing exams but one that will also teach you how to be a good therapist.

Consider the following when evaluating an MFT program:

- What is the accreditation status of the program?

- What is the pass rate for its graduates in terms of the state licensing exams?

- Is the program well respected by local professionals and training centers?

- Is the MFT program part of a larger university?

- Is the program well funded?

- How long has the MFT program been in existence?

- What do past program graduates say about their experience?

- What are the educational backgrounds of the program's faculty?

- What types of resources does the program offer its students and alumni?

- Does the program meet all of the latest educational requirements as regulated by the state?

  For those in California, note that, at the time of this writing, the state board is significantly revising the educational requirements for MFT licensure and intern registration. For more details, see the website of California's state licensing board:

  www.bbs.ca.gov/bd_activity/mft_educ_comm_update.shtml

For additional considerations when evaluating an MFT program, see the suggested questions at the end of this chapter.

What Are Your Needs?

In choosing the best graduate school for yourself, think about what kind of lifestyle you (and your family, if applicable) want and need during your years of graduate school.

Ask for a tour of any programs that are of interest to you to get a feel for the campus, facilities, and program. Take note of current students to understand the type of student they're looking for and who would be your fellow classmates.

Some additional points to consider:

- Are you able to attend graduate school full-time, or do you need a program that offers the flexibility of part-time enrollment?

- Will you be working concurrently? If so, will the location of the program and the class schedule work for you?

- Are you able to relocate, or do you want/need to stay in your current residence?

- Do you want to live on-campus?

- Do you want to attend a large-scale university where there is a large undergraduate population, or do you prefer a commuter campus that is geared primarily toward adult learning?

Theoretical Orientation

As you will learn in your MFT program, there are many theoretical models of counseling and psychology. These different schools of thought influence clinicians to approach their clients in a particular way.

Some MFT programs emphasize a particular theoretical orientation. For example, one MFT program might lean toward short-term psychodynamic therapies and cognitive-behavioral based treatments. Another might highlight transpersonal or humanistic principles.

Although you will get an introduction to many models of thought during your MFT education, your program's orientation may influence what or how course material is discussed in your classes. A school's theoretical orientation may also attract faculty members who have complementary research interests.

This theoretical orientation may be an undercurrent throughout your education. If possible, it is a good idea to choose a school that has a similar viewpoint to your own. Not sure which theoretical orientation fits you? Do not worry. Your MFT education will enable you to choose which theory best fits who you are and want to be as an MFT.

A school will usually make their theoretical orientation well-known on their website and marketing materials but, if they do not or you are not sure, just ask.

Location, location, location!

Just as with buying a home, think carefully about choosing a graduate school that is in the best location for your needs. These needs will be different for everyone, so there is no right or wrong.

MFT graduate programs consist of class work and fieldwork. Your fieldwork is a clinical placement during which you will be a therapist to real clients.

Yes, it is both exciting and scary to sit with your first clients but, do not worry, you will be learning what to do in your classes and will have a supervisor with whom to talk about your cases. These topics will be discussed more in future chapters.

For now, just know that, while you are in graduate school, you will also be seeing clients. Usually, you will see these clients at an off-campus agency that is not associated with your school, i.e. you will need to apply and interview for your fieldwork placement.

How does this affect you while you are deciding where to apply? Think about the location of each graduate school and what types of opportunities exist for these placements.

Many rural campuses do not have a lot of options for fieldworks, while urban campuses will have several. On the flip side, most rural areas do not have a lot of MFT programs. Therefore, there will be less competition for these placements.

Make a List

In deciding where you are going to apply, make a list of questions that you want answered before applying. After all, why go to the trouble of applying to a school only to find out during the interview stage that it does not offer something that you need or want?

TIP: DO YOUR RESEARCH NOW.

Call the programs in which you are interested, and ask them your list of questions. Take notes!

A sample script with suggested questions is included below:

"Hello, I am interested in applying to your Marriage and Family Therapy graduate program. I have a few questions about your program. May I please speak with the MFT program manager?"

When you are speaking with the MFT program manager, have a list of questions ready. Be thorough, as you want to collect as much data as possible to assist you in your decision on where to apply.

Some suggested questions:

- What percentage of your graduates passes their licensing exams on the first try?

- What is the average age of an MFT student in your program?

- Does your program offer both part-time and full-time enrollment? How many students are enrolled full-time versus part-time?

- How long does the average MFT student take to complete your program? What is the shortest amount of time in which a student can graduate?

- Are students in your program allowed to take any classes off-campus in order to graduate faster? If so, is there a limit as to how many classes?

- Are there any additional courses that would be required for state licensure after graduating from your program?

- As part of an MFT program, I understand that I will take classes and see clients in a clinical placement. Does your program offer an on-campus clinical placement? If not, does your program offer assistance for finding a clinical placement?

- Are the majority of your students able to find paid placements as an MFT Trainee? How about as an MFT Intern?

- What types of resources does your program offer to alumni?

- For those in California: I understand that the state board is significantly revising the educational requirements for MFT licensure and intern registration. Has your program addressed these changes? If not, how does your program plan on addressing these changes, and what is the projected timeline for the implementation of these new requirements?

  For more details on these proposed changes, see the BBS' website:

  www.bbs.ca.gov/bd_activity/mft_educ_comm_update.shtml

Chapter 6
Applying to Graduate School

You have decided where you want to apply. Just like in college, do not forget your safety school. Try to apply to a few different programs so you cover your bases and have some choices.

The Interview

Though it is natural to be nervous, remember that you are interviewing them as much as they are interviewing you. While you both want to make a good impression, take this opportunity to get a feel for whether you think the program is a good "fit" for you.

- Be prepared. Read about the school before the interview. Check the program's website to read about their faculty. Pick one or two faculty members whose area of research particularly interests you so that you can speak about your interest during the interview.

- Dress professionally. For men and women, a conservative suit is always best. Show that you are serious about yourself and your career potential.

- Bring a briefcase with a notepad and pen to take notes. Remember, these notes will be important once you are sitting down with your acceptances and deciding where you want to go.

- Have a few questions ready to ask your interviewers to show your interest in their program. Review the questions at the end of Chapter 5 for ideas.

- Find out when they will notify candidates of their acceptances. (This question is important both to manage your anxiety and for sending a thank you note, which is discussed below.)

- Remember to smile.

You may be interviewed in both a group setting as well as individually. Following are some typical interview questions with sample answers:

1. **Question**: If you are not married, how do you think that might affect your being a Marriage and Family Therapist?

Answer: Although I am not married, I have had many interpersonal relationships in my life and have faced issues such as financial pressures, blending two lives, and learning to manage conflict. This perspective will help me assist others with their unique challenges.

2. **Question**: What are your weaknesses?

   Answer: I take my work home. In becoming a therapist, I will need to learn strong emotional boundaries so that I don't get weighed down by my client's issues or experience emotional burnout.

3. **Question**: What are your strengths?

   Answer: I am a good listener. I have often been called "the therapist" among my friends. I really enjoy helping people and look forward to strengthening my listening skills in graduate school.

4. **Question**: Why do you want to attend our program?

   Answer: I am very impressed with the quality of both students and professors. There are several professors here who have published research that is of interest to me. For example, [full name] and [his/her] work on [the link between depression and relationship distress].

Get the idea? For every question, find an answer that both answers the question and relates to your future career potential in a positive way.

You may also be given a brief case study and be asked questions about what you think or how you would handle certain aspects of the case. Don't worry; they do not expect you to have all of the answers. They know you are not an MFT yet. They just want to get a baseline understanding of your thinking.

Thank You Notes

When you get back home, send a brief thank you note within one day to everyone with whom you interviewed. Include something you discussed to jog their memory about you and to make it more personal.

See Appendix A for two sample thank you notes.

Email or snail mail? The answer depends on how quickly the acceptance committee will be making their decision. Since you asked for this information during the interview, base your decision on that answer. If there will be a quick turnaround, it is ok to email your thank you note.

Better for them to receive an email before their decision than a written note afterward.

You Got In!

A note when you are considering your acceptance(s). First, congratulations! Second, remember to choose the best "fit" for you.

> TIP: THE BEST CHOICE FOR YOU MAY NOT BE YOUR FIRST INSTINCT OR WHERE OTHERS ARE ENCOURAGING YOU TO GO.

Get the notes you took during your interviews and campus tours, and make a pro/con list for every school where you have been accepted.

What were your general impressions? How do the schools compare in terms of the questions in Chapter 5? Which program best fits you and would most motivate you? Which school is most convenient? Which program is most affordable?

My Own Story

I applied to a few MFT programs around the country. I was accepted at a prestigious COAMFTE-accredited program at a large university where, no doubt, I would have received a solid education and preparation as an MFT. However, I chose to attend a small, well-respected, local program for the following reasons:

- I knew I would make many professional connections during graduate school, and I wanted these connections to be located where I thought I would eventually want to settle and open my own practice.

- I wanted to remain in my community where I had a good support network, as I knew training to be a therapist would be both challenging and time-consuming.

- This program was highly regarded by its alumni and other local MFTs.

- This program had high pass rates for the state licensing exams.

- I wanted to remain living near my aging parents.

So, although I was attracted to the prestige and "collegiate feel" of the university program, the other factors were ultimately more important to me. I know I made the right choice for myself and received an exceptional education that also fit my needs at the time.

Your Needs

I encourage you to be honest with yourself about what program best fits your current needs.

My current needs are:

_____

_____

_____

_____

The needs of my family members are:

_____

_____

_____

_____

The school(s) that best matches my needs is:

_____

_____

_____

_____

The school(s) that best matches my family's needs is:

_____

_____

_____

_____

Chapter 7
You're In!

Congratulations on choosing the best MFT graduate program for yourself. Graduate school is an important time in your life. These years ahead of you will supply you not only with the knowledge needed to pass the MFT licensing exams but also with the unique opportunity to better understand yourself and your own family of origin dynamics.

Program Manager

Make friends with your MFT program manager. S/he keeps you on track, oversees the complexities of the MFT process, and will often be the one to help you find a fieldwork site.

Schedule a meeting with your graduate program manager within the first two weeks of school. Discuss your projected graduation date, so that s/he can assist you in planning your coursework to meet your goals.

Although the average MFT student completes his/her coursework in three years of full-time study, tailor your program to your needs. I completed my coursework in two and a half years, and I know others who did it in two years. Others may graduate in four or five years due to part-time enrollment or other life circumstances, such as pregnancy, family, or health issues.

Determine what will work best for you, and work with your program manager on how best to reach your goals.

CURRICULUM
When considering courses to take at the beginning of your MFT program, choose the courses that will best prepare you to start your fieldwork, such as the counseling technique courses and ethics and law.

ORGANIZATION
Get a good-looking file box (inflammable!), and set up files for all of your fieldwork and state licensing board forms. Make copies of all forms you hand into your educational institution. Get needed signatures from fieldwork supervisors in a timely manner (they could move, get pregnant, or disappear!). Save copies of all of your syllabi. You'll need them if you move to another state and want to get licensed there.

YOUR OWN PERSONAL PSYCHOTHERAPY
Choose your psychotherapist well. Regard your personal psychotherapy requirement as an opportunity not only to experience what it's like to be a client but also to support you through your program. Lots of issues come up as you move through a training program, and you need the support of a good therapist. A Psychology Master's program is very different from a Master's in History!

THE FUTURE
Start your networking from day one. Be cooperative and not competitive with classmates, faculty, fieldwork supervisors, etc. You never know when one of your colleagues from your MFT program might become the director of a new program or agency and needs to hire all new staff. You'll want to be the first one she/he thinks of to hire!

~ Ginia Laudisio, Program Manager,
Department of Counseling Psychology,
Dominican University of California

Classes

- Go to class. A lot of what you will learn about being a good therapist happens in class, not just from reading your textbooks.

- Do the work. While your end goal is being a successful MFT, you first need to pass the licensing exams. To do that, you need to learn the material.

  There is a lot of reading involved in learning how to be an MFT, and you will be writing a lot of papers. The time and effort you spend now will pay off when you start to see clients, are studying for the exams, and after you get licensed.

TIP: WHETHER YOU WERE A GOOD STUDENT IN COLLEGE OR SKIPPED EVERY OTHER CLASS, TURN A FRESH PAGE IN GRADUATE SCHOOL. AFTER YOU ARE LICENSED, YOU DO NOT WANT TO BE SITTING WITH A CLIENT THINKING "WOW, I WISH I HAD PAID ATTENTION IN THAT CLASS SO I KNOW WHAT TO DO NOW."

- Know what will be on your state licensing exams. Again, remember to keep your eye on passing your state's licensing exams. Take a look at your state licensing board's website now to gain an understanding of the content areas of your licensing exams.

  For California, these areas are:

  - Clinical Evaluation
  - Crisis Management
  - Treatment Planning
  - Treatment
  - Ethics
  - Law

Knowing that you will need to be proficient in all of these areas will give you a head's up in your studies.

- Start thinking about your practice specialty (also called a "niche") now. After you become licensed, it is a good idea to choose a specialty for your practice. There are thousands of therapists out there, and differentiating yourself is an important step toward success.

Take notice now of what you are drawn to in your reading and classes so you can start to get ideas about your niche.

Do you get excited reading about cognitive behavioral theory? Are you enjoying reading about working with children? Maybe you will want to specialize in cognitive behavioral therapy with children. Now is the time to start getting ideas so you can be one step ahead of your competition once you are ready to hang your shingle.

See Appendix B for a list of sample practice niches.

> TIP: START A JOURNAL TITLED "MY MFT PRACTICE" WHERE YOU CAN JOT DOWN THEORIES AND/OR CLASSES YOU LIKE AND DISLIKE, CLINICAL POPULATIONS IN WHICH YOU ARE INTERESTED, AND POSSIBLE AREAS OF SPECIALTY FOR THE FUTURE. THESE NOTES WILL BE INVALUABLE TO YOU WHEN YOU START LOOKING FOR YOUR FIRST FIELDWORK PLACEMENT AND AGAIN AFTER YOU GET LICENSED.

- Be prepared. Be sure to keep the course descriptions and syllabi from all of your classes. You may need them when applying for licensure or if you apply for licensure in a different state.

> TIP: YOU MAY BE REQUIRED TO TAKE ADDITIONAL COURSEWORK TO BE ELIGIBLE FOR STATE LICENSURE. START TAKING THESE COURSES NOW, OR DURING YOUR SUMMERS, TO GET LICENSED FASTER.

Letters of Recommendation

Ask for letters of recommendation from your professors after you complete a class. These recommendations will be useful when you are trying to secure your fieldwork and internships.

Writing a recommendation takes time. Offer to write a draft that your professors can then edit in whatever way they see fit. Email this draft or put it on a disk so it is easy for them to cut and paste it onto their letterhead.

TIP: PROFESSORS ARE BUSY, SO MAKE AS POSSIBLE FOR THEM TO WRITE YOU A RECOMMENDATION.

Organization

Being an MFT entails a lot of paperwork. You will get a taste for this aspect of being a therapist during graduate school, so it is important to learn good organization skills now.

For some of your graduate classes, you will receive a form called a "Certificate of Completion" at the end of the class. Beware: This is not some extraneous piece of paper you can lose. Keep it in a safe place, and make a copy that you keep in a different location. You will need to send this form into your state licensing board with your application for licensure.

Create a filing system (and use it) to stay organized. Create a label for the following file folders:

1. Expenses (all expenses related to graduate school)

2. Papers (copies of class papers you want to keep)

3. Certificates of Completion

4. Letters of Recommendation

5. FW Sites (information about fieldworks in which you might be interested, copies of your fieldwork applications, etc.)

6. Assessment Forms (for assessment instruments you receive in class, which you will use during your fieldwork and after you are licensed)

You will be adding several more files in Chapter 15, so be sure to create a filing system large enough to keep everything in one place.

Make Friends

Some people approach graduate school as being a place exclusively for learning, rather than a place where both learning and friendship can occur.

The study and practice of psychotherapy is both personally and professionally challenging. The nature of the profession can be lonely and isolating, so embrace the friendships you can make during graduate school.

> TIP: THERE WILL BE FEW TIMES IN YOUR LIFE WHERE YOU WILL BE SURROUNDED BY OTHERS WITH SUCH SIMILAR INTERESTS, SO TAKE ADVANTAGE OF IT.

Remember that your fellow students will become your professional colleagues down the road. You will be consulting with them, referring clients to them, and (hopefully) receiving referrals from them. You will also support each other emotionally, now and as practicing MFTs, so be professional, friendly, and supportive of each other during graduate school.

Psychotherapy is a unique profession. You will find that it is beneficial to have friends in the business who understand the intricacies of your work.

Share Your Experience

When I was in graduate school, the professor in my first class announced that those who were currently married might find themselves getting divorced over the course of the program. He explained this shift often occurs due to the personal growth MFT students experience and the fact that spouses are usually not going through the same internal changes.

He encouraged us to speak with our significant others and include them in our learning so that we would grow together. Though I was not married at the time, I remember looking around to newly formed friends who were married and seeing temperatures and nerves rising.

Moral of the story: talk to your spouse, and include him or her in the personal growth you will be undergoing throughout your training years.

Working Concurrently

Many of you will need to work while attending graduate school. If this is the case, here are some important points to remember:

- Balance: Maintain a reasonable schedule. Explore going to school part-time if needed.

- Self-care: Part of being a good therapist is taking care of yourself. Exercise regularly, eat well, get enough sleep, go to your own therapy, and take frequent mental breaks from all things therapy.

- Ask for help. You will be stretching yourself thin by working while attending graduate school. Do not be afraid to let others help you manage it all.

- Put your Blackberry or iPhone away during class. When you are in class, it can be tempting to try to stay on top of your workload by multi-tasking.

  Although your attention may need to be split at times, try to put your mobile devices away when in class.

  Let yourself concentrate on school when you are in school and on work when you are at work.

Working full time and going to graduate school is remarkable work! It requires the delicate management of sacrifice, fear, labor, persistence, perseverance, depth and accomplishment. Remind yourself that these extreme efforts will strengthen the core values that will later be drawn upon to provide an invaluable service to others and to yourself. Often times, it helped me to frame the joining of these two challenges, as not just necessary for survival, but as an opportunity for me to expand in my therapeutic training experience.

~ Melyssa Nelson, MFT, Private Practice, San Francisco

While in graduate school, get to know your authentic self, i.e. the real you. If therapists don't do their own personal work through their own therapy, then they are unable to get to know their own "hot buttons" and will not be as beneficial to their clients. Also, take care of yourself. Spend some time taking breaks and doing something that you love as much as psychotherapy, so you can fill up your tank every now and then.

~ Dianne Kraaijvanger, LMFT, LMHC, Boston

Chapter 8
Professional Associations

There are several professional organizations to which therapists can belong. Some are specific to Marriage and Family Therapists, while others include both MFTs and other therapy professionals.

The primary organizations for MFTs consist of the following:

- American Association of Marriage and Family Therapy (AAMFT) www.aamft.org

- Your state association of Marriage and Family Therapy

  For example, California's state association is called the California Association of Marriage and Family Therapists (CAMFT). www.camft.org

You may be wondering if you should become a member of these professional associations before you are licensed. The answer is: if you can afford it, yes! These associations offer invaluable resources to both pre-licensed and licensed MFTs.

California's state association, for example, has three particularly valuable resources to note:

1. CAMFT pre-licensed and licensed members have access to an attorney who specializes in Marriage and Family Therapy. As a member, you can call CAMFT and speak to this attorney about any legal issue concerning your practice. Take advantage of this resource. If you have a question, call! Always document the name of the attorney with whom you spoke, the date, and any advice that was given.

2. CAMFT's website has a section devoted to pre-licensed members called the "Prelicensees' Corner." Here, you can find helpful articles about clinical matters, the experience of being a trainee or intern, taking the exams, and other relevant matters.

3. CAMFT has an online networking and discussion forum called the "CAMFT

Member's List Serve" for both pre-licensed and licensed members. Members post case questions and other topics relevant to the practice of Marriage and Family Therapy in California.

Below is a sample of additional organizations that you may want to explore depending on your clinical interests.

Take a moment to review their websites to find out exactly what benefits you will receive as a member and how much membership costs. Many of these associations also have a lot of free information available on their website.

> TIP: THE COSTS OF PROFESSIONAL MEMBERSHIPS CAN ADD UP, SO PRIORITIZE JOINING THOSE THAT OFFER YOU A THERAPIST DIRECTORY LISTING. THIS LISTING WILL SERVE AS ADVERTISING FOR YOU WHEN SOMEONE FROM THE PUBLIC IS LOOKING FOR A THERAPIST.

- Sandplay Therapists of America
  www.sandplay.org

- American Art Therapy Association
  www.arttherapy.org

- Association for Pet Loss and Bereavement
  www.aplb.org

- Association for Play Therapy
  www.a4pt.org

- National Association for Drama
  Therapy
  www.nadt.org

- Association for Behavioral and
  Cognitive Therapies
  www.aabt.org

- American Dance Therapy Association
  www.adta.org

- International Expressive Arts Therapy
  Association
  www.ieata.org

- American Music Therapy Association
  www.musictherapy.org

- Therapy Dogs International
  www.tdi-dog.org

- American Horticultural Therapy
  Association
  www.ahta.org

- American Psychotherapy and Medical
  Hypnosis Association
  www.apmha.com

- International Family Therapy
  Association
  www.ifta-familytherapy.org

- American Group Psychotherapy Assoc.
  www.agpa.org

> TIP: ASK ABOUT AVAILABLE STUDENT RATES AND
> DISCOUNTS.

Gaining early exposure to the various clinical opportunities available to you before or after licensure will place you one step ahead come time to open your practice or find a job as a licensed MFT.

Chapter 9
Taxes, Part I

Note: The information in this chapter does not represent tax advice and should not be assumed to be free of errors. When in doubt, contact the IRS, a tax accountant, or an income tax service.

M ost payments that are received by graduate students for either assistantships or fellowships are considered taxable income by the federal government.

If you have received a scholarship for graduate school, be sure to consult with the IRS, a tax accountant, or an income tax service regarding what part of the scholarship can be excluded as income. Generally, student loans are not considered taxable income.

Learn what types of tax deductions are available to you while you are in graduate school. Ask your tax accountant, or do some research on the Internal Revenue Service's website: www.irs.gov.

You may be eligible to claim a federal "Hope Tax Credit" for tuition and related expenses. You may also be eligible to claim the Lifetime Learning Credit on your taxes.

> TIP: ASK YOUR TAX ACCOUNTANT WHETHER YOU QUALIFY FOR THE HOPE CREDIT AND/OR THE LIFETIME LEARNING CREDIT.

SECTION THREE:
Getting the Hours

Chapter 10
On Being A Trainee

Note: In California, a pre-degree individual who is currently enrolled in an MFT graduate program is called an "MFT Trainee." Post-degree, s/he is called an "MFT Intern." For the purposes of this book, I will be using the California MFT terminology, so be sure to check with your state licensing board for the corresponding terms and requirements.

The time has come to start seeing your very first clients in a clinical placement, which I will call "fieldwork." You are probably feeling excited, nervous, and curious. All of these feelings are normal and will be explored further in Chapter 14.

For now, accept that you are not expected to know exactly what to do, and you will learn. Just trust that you are ready for this learning, and be patient with yourself.

TIP: REVIEW THE STATE LICENSING EXAM MATERIALS.

You may be thinking, "Why in the world would I start studying for my exams now?" Do not worry, I am not suggesting that you start studying for your exams now. I am also not suggesting that you buy the exam materials at this point because they are very expensive and will probably be updated by the time you are ready to study for your exams.

Reading the exam material at this point can, however, be extremely helpful in preparing you to see clients. The study materials effectively consolidate what you are learning. In addition, since you will begin to see clients before you have taken all of your classes, the material will also give you a good overview of what you have not yet studied.

For example, are you anxious about the legal and ethical requirements you must follow when seeing clients? The exam materials will lay out exactly what you need to know so you do not have to wade through your class textbook trying to piece together what you need to know and/or do in certain situations.

The exam materials will not tell you everything you need to know to pass your classes or to be a good therapist. They will give you the nuts and bolts of the most important things to remember while starting to see clients, something that can be very beneficial to the new therapist just starting out.

Where do you get these materials? Many newly licensed therapists will donate their exam materials to their schools, training centers, or advertise them online.

> *I love the work. Sometimes people ask if it is depressing to spend all day listening to problems. I tell them, "I am not listening to problems. I am listening for solutions."*
> *~ Mary Pipher,*
> Letters To A Young Therapist

Chapter 11
Choosing the Best Fieldwork Site

The first step is to decide where you will see clients. Where do you want to work? With whom? As you will discover, there are a variety of fieldwork placements available, so you want to pick the best one for you.

How do you know which site is the best for you? Reflect on your long-term goals. What do you want to do with your MFT license?

Knowing your MFT goals will assist you in knowing where to apply for your fieldwork placement.

TIP: READ CHAPTERS 31, 34 AND APPENDIX B TO START EXPLORING CAREER AND NICHE IDEAS.

My MFT Goals:

_____

_____

_____

_____

_____

Think about how the sites you are considering will provide you with the necessary training and experience to get you closer to your goals.

> TIP: AT THE BEGINNING OF YOUR TRAINING YEARS, IT IS A GOOD IDEA TO WORK SOMWHERE WHERE YOU WILL BE EXPOSED TO A VARIETY OF CLIENT POPULATIONS AND PROBLEMS.

Where To Look

The second step is finding the job. Your MFT program may or may not help you find your fieldwork placement. If they do help you, this help may take the form of setting it all up for you so that all you have to do is show up or, more likely, they may simply hand you a list of nearby agencies that employ MFT Trainees and the rest is up to you.

Whether you get a little or no help, do not panic. There are plenty of agencies looking for free help, and that is where you come in! That is right, I said free. Chances are, you will not get paid. If you are paid, it likely won't be much. This fact is important to know upfront so that you can plan and budget.

So – where do you look for these agencies if you have to start from scratch? The best resource is your fellow students. Ask those ahead of you in your program where they worked, if they got paid, whether they liked it, and any suggestions for applying.

Another option is to search online for "mental health agencies," "mental health services," "social service agencies," "counseling centers," "counseling services," or "mental health clinics" in your area. You can also find listings in the yellow pages. When you call any of these listings, ask if they employ MFT Trainees.

Chapter 12
Applying to a Fieldwork Site

Once you narrow down where and with whom you are interested in working, find out the application process for each of your prospective fieldwork sites.

> TIP: MANY FIELDWORK SITES ONLY ACCEPT APPLICATIONS ONCE OR TWICE A YEAR, SO PLAN AHEAD.

Just like for graduate school, you will most likely need to interview. Find out the format of the interview ahead of time so you are prepared, and review the interview suggestions again in Chapter 6.

Once again, remember that now is the time to ascertain whether you feel like the site is a match, both to your personality and to your clinical needs.

Some specific considerations to explore for each site include:

- **Finances:** Will you be paid? If so, will you be paid hourly, or will you receive a percentage of your client fees? Do you need to pay the fieldwork site for anything?

- **The theoretical orientation of the site:** Many training centers that employ MFT Trainees and MFT Interns have a specific theoretical orientation. Make sure it works for you.

  If you want to learn more about cognitive behavioral theory, you probably do not want to work in a psychodynamically-oriented site. If you are not spiritually or religiously inclined, you may feel uncomfortable in a site that incorporates spiritual or religious traditions in their trainings and clinical approach to cases.

- **Client population:** What population does the site serve, and does this population interest you? Are their clients primarily adults, children, economically disadvantaged, SED, etc.?

  As already mentioned, it is a good idea to work somewhere where you will be exposed to many different types of clientele and clinical issues your first fieldwork placement.

This early exposure will help you learn with what problems and with what populations you like to work. Both of these are important in helping you to define your future clinical niche. Even if you think you already know with whom and what you like to work, you may surprise yourself.

- **Supervision:** Do they offer group and/or individual supervision? How are supervisors assigned? What happens if you want to switch supervisors? Do you need to pay for supervision?

- **Location:** You will be traveling to this site several days per week, so make sure your commute and the parking situation will not drive you crazy.

- **Schedule:** Fieldwork sites usually require weekly meetings for all of the MFT Trainees and/or MFT Interns to discuss cases, to participate in trainings, and to offer professional support. Some also require participation in yearly retreats, spring-cleaning days, or other group activities. Find out the weekly and yearly schedule and exactly what is required of you.

- **Trainings:** What types of trainings are offered? Are these on-site or off-site? Are they required? What is the training schedule?

- **Cases:** How are cases distributed? What happens if you are assigned a case that you do not want? Is there a minimum caseload that you are expected to handle? What happens if you exceed or do not meet this number?

- **Office space:** How is office space handled? Have they had any past problems with having enough office space available? Will office space be available to you when you are available to work? For example, if your schedule only allows you to see clients in the mornings or in the evenings, will office space be available to you during these times?

- **Your colleagues:** Does this site employ only Master's level professionals, or do they also hire doctoral-level candidates? Can you see yourself learning from and being interested in your colleagues?

- **Commitment:** What type of commitment is required? Most sites require a one-year commitment. Can you stay longer if desired? If you want to leave before your contract expires, what happens? Whenever you leave, can you take your clients with you?

The Decision Is Made

Congratulations! Another important step on the road to becoming an MFT has been made. You have a job!

Chapter 13
Supervision

Before you see any clients, you will need a supervisor. Since you are not yet licensed, you cannot practice without supervision. You will meet weekly with your supervisor to discuss your cases, either individually or in a group format.

Tip: Choose your supervisor carefully.

This person will be your mentor and will have a strong impact on your early development as a therapist. Yes, you will survive and learn even if you do not feel a strong match with your supervisor, but the amount of growth available to you when you are well matched is profound.

Supervision is also an important time to further increase your understanding of material that will be on your exams. It is important to choose a supervisor who is dedicated to your learning, familiar with exam content, and open to questions.

> TIP: IF YOU ARE GOING TO MOVE OUT OF STATE BEFORE YOU ARE FINISHED WITH YOUR HOURS OR MAY WISH TO GET LICENSED IN A DIFFERENT STATE, GETTING ALL OF YOUR SUPERVISION FROM AN AAMFT APPROVED SUPERVISOR MAY MINIMIZE PROBLEMS WITH TRANSFERRING YOUR HOURS.

Some additional points to consider:

- Think about the past bosses you have had. With what type of personality do you work best?

- Do you want someone well-versed in a particular theory (e.g. Control Mastery Theory, Cognitive Behavioral Theory, etc)?

- Do you want someone who specializes in a certain population (e.g. children, adolescents, eating disorders, domestic violence)?

- Is your supervisor's gender important to you?

- Where is the potential supervisor's office located? Usually, you will be meeting at his or her office. Is the office conveniently located for you?

- Are there past supervisees with whom you can speak to get their impression of the supervisor's style?

> TIP: WHETHER YOU ARE TECHNICALLY ALLOWED TO "CHOOSE" YOUR SUPERVISOR OR NOT, BE SURE TO SHARE YOUR PREFERENCES WITH WHOEVER IS IN CHARGE OF ASSIGNING SUPERVISORS.

Meeting Your Supervisor

When you first meet with your supervisor, help him or her understand what it is you need from him or her. Take a moment to think about what you want to communicate to your supervisor.

What is your style of learning?

_____

_____

_____

_____

_____

_____

What are particular items on which you want to focus in supervision?

_____

_____

_____

_____

_____

_____

What are your current clinical concerns?

_____

_____

_____

_____

_____

_____

My Story

In my first supervision, I found my anxiety over crisis situations was very high. I needed my supervisor to walk me through (several different times) exactly what I would do if a client was suicidal, homicidal, or shared something about child or elder abuse.

When I was in my second fieldwork placement working with a different supervisor, I found that I wanted support around finding my own voice as a clinician. Whereas I needed my first supervisor to often "tell me what to do," I was ready to start figuring it out for myself by the time I was working with my second supervisor.

During my first supervision session with this second supervisor, I shared:

"When I am presenting a case to you, I know my tendency will be to ask for your advice before exploring my own thoughts. This tendency comes from my own anxiety and insecurity about being a good therapist.

With your assistance, I would like to work on developing my own voice as a therapist. So, would you please encourage me to tell you what I would do in a situation before offering what you would do?"

My supervisor really appreciated hearing what I needed and, in working with this supervisor, I was able to begin the discovery of my own voice and gain the self-confidence I needed as a therapist.

TIP: YOUR SUPERVISOR'S LICENSE MUST BE ACTIVE AND IN GOOD STANDING FOR YOUR HOURS TO COUNT TOWARD LICENSURE. CHECK WITH YOUR STATE LICENSING BOARD TO VERIFY THE STATUS OF YOUR SUPERVISOR'S LICENSE. YOU CAN OFTEN VERIFY LICENSES ONLINE, SO CHECK YOUR STATE BOARD'S WEBSITE.

Supervisor Issues

What if you do not like your supervisor or feel like you are not getting what you need in your supervision?

First, try to pinpoint exactly what is not working for you. Then, similar to what you will encourage your clients to do when they want to stop therapy for whatever reason, I encourage you to talk with your supervisor about your feelings.

Broaching such a subject can be scary and intimidating, but you owe it to yourself to see if this working relationship can be re-worked so that it works for you.

Regardless of the outcome, talking about the interpersonal issues between you and your therapist will be greatly beneficial for you as a person and a clinician.

> TIP: IF YOU HAVE TALKED WITH YOUR SUPERVISOR ALREADY OR THE PROBLEM IS NOT SOMETHING THAT CAN BE CHANGED, THEN GIVE YOURSELF PERMISSION TO REQUEST A CHANGE OF SUPERVISORS.

Do not be afraid to take this step. You are meeting with this person for two reasons only, and that is to help you manage your cases and to learn to be a therapist. If there is something that is preventing these things from happening, then it is in your best interest and your clients' best interests to find a supervisor with whom you work well.

Talk to the director at your fieldwork placement, and explain to him/her the situation and your request. Such a request is not uncommon. If need be, feel free to ask the program manager of your MFT program to assist you in securing alternative supervision.

My best advice for unlicensed MFTs in supervision is to really challenge yourself. Go outside of your comfort level, and push yourself to experiment with the things you learn in the classroom. It is one of the only times that you have such a tremendous support system to ask questions and try on new hats. I also think videotaping is what made me as strong of a clinician as I am today. It was painful to watch myself, but it was priceless in observing myself and improving on my shortcomings as well as my strengths. I would not have changed that for the world.

~ Dianne Kraaijvanger, LMFT, LMHC,
Boston

If you want to get the most out of supervision, you need either live supervision where your supervisor watches you work with a family or you need to show your supervisor videotapes of your work with families.

~ Daniel Minuchin, MA, LMFT, AAMFT
Approved Supervisor, Senior Faculty Member
at the Minuchin Center for the Family,
New York

Chapter 14
Seeing Clients

Starting to see your first clients can be an exciting, scary, and anxiety-ridden event. Explore your feelings in your personal therapy and with your supervisor. It is also a good idea to seek the support of both your fellow graduate school classmates and fieldwork peers. Remember, you are all in the same boat!

> Waiting for my very first client, I rehearsed how best to convey unconditional positive regard. How did my own therapist do it? What would my supervisor suggest?
>
> I moved the therapist's chair a little to the left, then back again. I wished there was nicer art on the walls. I checked the

> waiting room several times. I told myself to breathe.
>
> Would my client know I was as green as I felt?
>
> What would I say if she asked how many clients I'd seen before?

Mental Preparation

Thinking about seeing my first clients, I feel:

_____

_____

_____

_____

_____

_____

_____

I am most concerned about:

_____

_____

_____

_____

_____

_____

_____

_____

When you first begin seeing clients, you may find yourself invigorated by the experience, bubbling over with energy and wanting to devote as much time as possible to living and breathing the work. On the other hand, you may also find yourself emotionally and mentally exhausted at the end of the day.

Either way, be patient with yourself. You are learning a new skill, and it takes time to achieve the balance needed to sustain this type of work.

Self-Care

The MFT profession can be emotionally draining. You will need to practice self-care regularly throughout your career to prevent emotional burnout. Self-care is also important to model to your clients.

Take the time now to begin practicing the following self-care tools:

- Take quiet time to yourself.

- Exercise regularly.

- Eat healthily.

- Seek the company of supportive friends and family.

- Spend time with friends outside the field.

- Get adequate sleep.

- Go to your own therapy.

- Let yourself (or make yourself) take a break from all things therapy.

- Do not let yourself become so depleted that you do not have time to devote to other people and things that you love.

Too often, we therapists neglect our personal relationships. Our work becomes our life. At the end of our workday, having given so much of ourselves, we feel drained of desire for more relationship.

Besides, patients are so grateful, so adoring, so idealizing, we therapists run the risk of becoming less appreciative of family members and friends, who fail to recognize our omniscience and excellence in all things.
~ *Irvin Yalom,* The Gift of Therapy

Your Therapist Hat

Be conscious of taking off your therapy hat at the end of each day. This skill is important, both for your personal relationships as well as for your own sanity. Friends and family will be sensitive to being "therapized" or analyzed, and you will need this time off.

TIP: ADD WHAT YOU ARE LEARNING ABOUT YOURSELF FROM YOUR WORK WITH CLIENTS TO THE MFT JOURNAL YOU STARTED IN CHAPTER 7. REMEMBER TO PROTECT YOUR CLIENTS' CONFIDENTIALITY AND NEVER WRITE DOWN ANY IDENTIFYING INFORMATION ABOUT ANY OF YOUR CLIENTS. MAKE THIS JOURNAL ABOUT YOUR EXPERENCES, NOT ABOUT YOUR CLIENTS.

Chapter 15
Paperwork

There is a lot of paperwork along the road to becoming an MFT. Again, it is about being organized from the beginning. In this chapter, you will begin to create an organizational system that will be in place until after you are licensed.

What Are All of These Forms?

It is your responsibility to stay on top of your licensing state's latest requirements. For California, as of this writing, there are three main forms. You may view them by going to the website of the state licensing board, called the Board of Behavioral Sciences: www.bbs.ca.gov.

Let's review each individually:

1. MFT Supervisor Responsibility Statement: You will have one of these forms completed for every supervisor until you

are licensed. You will need to mail the original copies of these forms with your application for licensure. That could be many years away, so be sure not to lose them.

Bring this form to your supervisor to sign before you start seeing clients at the fieldwork site where s/he is supervising you.

2. MFT Weekly Summary of Hours of Experience: This form accounts for every single professional hour until you are licensed. As you can imagine, by the time you are applying for licensure, you will have many of these forms for each fieldwork placement.

> TIP: KEEP YOUR PRE-DEGREE AND POST-DEGREE HOURS ON SEPARATE FORMS TO HELP YOU KEEP TRACK OF YOUR HOURS AND TO HELP YOUR STATE LICENSING BOARD PROCESS YOUR APPLICATION.

Technically, you are expected to have your supervisor sign this form every week. Many people get behind and only bring this form in to be signed once a month or so. I suggest you bring in your form every week to be signed, not just to follow the rules but to protect yourself. If something happens to your supervisor and s/he has not signed for your hours in two months, you are out of luck and will not be able to count those hours toward licensure. So stay on top of it!

At the time of this writing, you do not need to mail in these forms with your application packet for licensure. You will need the information on the forms, however, to complete your application.

Note: After you send in your application, you can get "audited" by the state board. If this happens, you will need to mail in all of these weekly hour forms so the board can verify your hours - so keep these forms safe until you are licensed!

3. MFT Experience Verification: You will have one of these forms completed for every supervisor until you are licensed. This form needs to be signed by your supervisor when you stop working with him/her OR when you stop working at the site where s/he was supervising you. Bring this form to your supervisor to sign on your last day of supervision. You will need to mail the original copy of this form in with your application for licensure.

> TIP: MINIMIZE YOUR SUPERVISOR'S WORKLOAD BY COMPLETING AS MUCH INFORMATION AS YOU CAN ON THE FORMS BEFORE THEY SIGN.

Protect Your Investment

> TIP: MAKE DUPLICATES OF ALL OF YOUR FORMS AND KEEP THEM IN DIFFERENT LOCATIONS.

I kept an updated set of all of my completed forms in two different locations until I was licensed: in a filing cabinet in my house and in a drawer at my parents' house. I also scanned one set of the forms and kept them on a disk.

Sound excessive? It is better to be safe than sorry, so protect yourself and all of your hard work. Your state licensing board is not going to make an exception to needing your forms because your dog ate them, they got lost in a fire, or they were in your car when it was stolen.

Where will you keep copies of your forms?

Organization

You will now be adding to the filing system you started in Chapter 7. You will create files for everything you will need from now through licensure.

For those who will be lic␣
you will create the following list
labels in total). For those who w␣
other states, you will create two la␣
your state-required forms and on␣ ␣r the
items numbered 6 - 12 below:

1. MFT Blank Forms (where you will keep blank copies of the next three forms)

2. MFT Supervisor Forms x 2 (keep sets in different locations)

3. MFT Hours Forms x 2 (keep sets in different locations)

4. MFT Verification Forms x 2 (keep sets in different locations)

5. MFT Intern Registration (keep a copy of anything you have sent into the board regarding your MFT Intern Registration)

6. Marketing (keep a copy of all marketing ideas you have, projects completed, expenses)

7. Website (all materials related to your professional website)

8. Networking (business cards of professionals you have met, copies of all correspondence you have sent to referral sources)

9. MFT Insurance (copies of proof of insurance, receipts)

10.MFT Exams (all items related to your exams, such as copies of practice exams, receipts for study materials, etc.)

11.MFT Application (a copy of everything you mail to your state's licensing board when sending in your licensure application)

12.CEUs (for use after licensure for your required Continuing Education)

Chapter 16
Watch Your Ratios

Every state requires a certain number of total hours to be completed prior to being licensed. These hours are divided into different categories. There are often a minimum and maximum number of hours allowed or required in each category.

For example, California requires 3,000 total hours. These hours consist of many different categories, such as adult therapy, child therapy, couples therapy, group therapy, trainings, telephone counseling, supervision, telemedicine, and hours spent doing paperwork.

In the next chapter, you will find charts for you to complete with your state licensing requirements. Take the time to complete these charts now because you will be referring to them often.

These charts will assist you in keeping track of what is or is not allowed in your state as you trudge your way through your hours. If you are not sure of any of the answers, call your state licensing board or professional association and ask them for the specific answers.

Remember, it is your responsibility to stay on top of your state licensing requirements, as they may change periodically.

Chapter 17
Chart Your State

Following are blank charts for you to complete with your state licensing requirements. Take the time to complete these charts now because you will be referring to them often as you progress through The Therapy Three.

If you have any questions, visit the website of your state licensing board for answers.

> TIP: CALIFORNIA'S STATE LICENSING BOARD HAS A HELPFUL OVERVIEW OF THEIR LICENSING PROCESS AND REQUIREMENTS ON THEIR WEBSITE:
> WWW.BBS.CA.GOV/APP-REG/MFT_REQUIREMENT.SHTML

MFT HOURS OF EXPERIENCE
FOR MY STATE

Clinical Experience

Experience Type (given by you)	Allowed Pre-Degree?	Allowed Post-Degree?	Minimums and Maximums	Notes
Individual Therapy				
Couples or Family Therapy				
Child Therapy				
Group Therapy				
Telephone Counseling				

Additional Notes:

_____

_____

_____

_____

Supervision

Experience Type	Allowed Pre-Degree?	Allowed Post-Degree?	Minimums and Maximums	Notes
Individual Supervision				
Group Supervision				

Additional Notes:

_____

_____

_____

_____

_____

_____

_____

_____

Other

Experience Type	Allowed Pre-Degree?	Allowed Post-Degree?	Minimums and Maximums	Notes
Personal Therapy (received by you)				
Writing Clinical Reports, Progress or Process Notes				
Attending Trainings, Workshops, Conferences				

Additional Notes:

_____

_____

_____

_____

_____

TOTALS

Experience Type	Minimums and Maximums	Notes
Weeks of Experience Required	Minimum # of weeks:	
Total Hours of Experience Required	Maximum # of Pre-Degree Hours: Minimum # of Post-Degree Hours Minimum # of TOTAL hours:	

Template: Board of Behavioral Sciences. "MFT Breakdown of Required Supervised Experience." <http://www.bbs.ca.gov>.

Additional Notes:

_____

_____

_____

_____

_____

There are a few points worth mentioning about the charts you have just completed.

- If your state limits the number of hours you can count for paperwork and trainings, as does California, expect to reach the maximum on these.

- If your state has a minimum number of hours required in any particular category, be sure to plan ahead. For example, California requires a minimum of 500 hours doing therapy with couples, families, and children.

Your minimums are important to stay aware of when you are choosing a fieldwork placement or an internship site to make sure you will be able to acquire the hours you need to meet these minimums.

TIP: TAKE NOTE OF THE MAXIMUM NUMBER OF PRE-DEGREE HOURS YOU ARE ALLOWED TO COUNT TOWARD LICENSURE. DO NOT GO OVER THIS NUMBER, OR YOU ARE BASICALLY WORKING FOR FREE! REMEMBER THAT YOUR HOURS ARE YOUR PRIMARY COMPENSATION.

Chapter 18
Personal Psychotherapy

M ost MFT state licensing boards allow applicants to count a certain number of personal psychotherapy hours toward licensure. Refer to the charts you completed in Chapter 17 for your state's information.

| TIP: MAX OUT ON PERSONAL THERAPY HOURS. |

When possible, it is a good idea to max out on these hours for the following reasons:

- You have a professional responsibility to "be on top of your own stuff" as a therapist. Think of going to your own therapy as a pre-requisite to becoming a good clinician.

- You get to experience first-hand what it is like to be a therapy client, which will assist you in being a better therapist to others. You would not want to go to a doctor who had never been a patient himself, would you?

- Every therapist has a unique style and particular clinical orientation. Gaining exposure to different styles will help you define your own style and preferences.

Try out different therapists and different formats. Go to individual therapy, try a group, and get some couples therapy. An added benefit of going to couples therapy is your significant other seeing what it is you are studying to become. This understanding can help minimize the mystery of your new direction.

- Personal psychotherapy hours are an easy way to get that much closer to finishing your hours.

In California, at the time of this writing, you are required to accumulate 3,000 total hours prior to application for licensure. As part of these 3,000 hours, you are allowed to count up to 300 hours of personal psychotherapy. In addition, every hour of personal psychotherapy counts as three hours. So, this 3:1 ratio means you only have to complete 100 hours of personal therapy to count them as 300 hours.

Therapists must be familiar with their own dark side and be able to empathize with all human wishes and impulses.

A personal therapy experience permits the student therapist to experience many aspects of the therapeutic process from the patient's seat: the tendency to idealize the therapist, the yearning for dependency, the gratitude toward a caring and attentive listener, the power granted to the therapist.

Young therapists must work through their own neurotic issues; they must learn to accept feedback, discover their own blind spots, and see themselves as others see them; they must appreciate their impact upon others and learn how to provide accurate feedback.

Lastly, psychotherapy is a psychologically demanding enterprise, and therapists must develop the awareness and inner strength to cope with the many occupational hazards inherent in it.

~ Irvin Yalom, The Gift of Therapy

Think you can't afford your own psychotherapy? Many psychotherapists and counseling centers offer sliding scale services to graduate students, so there are affordable options.

Remember, your clients are going to use financial strain as a reason not to come to therapy or to stop prematurely– so take the time to explore your own resistance so you can help clients with this issue down the road.

The expense of therapy is often seen as a luxury, especially during more challenging economic times, so your own management of this issue will prepare you for helping your clients manage this issue.

Chapter 19
Tracking Your Hours

Now that you know the what and when of counting your hours, it is time to determine how you will keep track of all of the hours you will be accumulating.

In California, you must have 3,000 total hours to be licensed. Part of the breakdown of these 3,000 hours is as follows:

- An unlimited amount of individual psychotherapy hours (given by you)

- A minimum of 500 hours doing therapy with couples, families, and children

- A maximum of 250 hours of telephone counseling

- A maximum of 125 hours conducting telemedicine

As an MFT Trainee in California, you must have one hour of supervision for every 5 client hours and are not allowed to count any time you spend writing up your cases. As an MFT Intern, you must have one hour of supervision for every 10 client hours and can count up to 250 hours of the time you spend on your case notes.

There are more details to counting hours in California, but you get the idea... Keeping track of your hours can make your head swim!

Regardless of your licensing state, keeping track of your hours is a confusing task. So what should you do?

> TIP: TAKE THE HEADACHE OUT OF KEEPING TRACK OF YOUR HOURS, AND USE A SOFTWARE PROGRAM THAT WILL DO IT FOR YOU.

There are several software programs available that will save you from the headache of having to calculate your hours. These programs will let you know exactly where you are in the process and how many more hours you have to go within each category.

A colleague of mine worked an extra six months getting her hours because she was calculating one of the ratios incorrectly. Another colleague sent in her application thinking she was done when the state licensing board rejected her application for not having enough hours.

Unfortunately, these mistakes are not uncommon. Protect yourself on this leg of the journey, and get some help from one of the programs listed below.

- www.TrackYourHours.com

- MFT Licensing Reporter: www.Arsene. com

- Your state licensing board's website

  For California:
  www.bbs.ca.gov/app-reg/exp_calc.shtml

Chapter 20
Professional Liability

Professional liability insurance is essentially malpractice insurance. If you are sued for services rendered or if a claim is filed against you in your professional capacity, professional liability insurance will cover you up to the limits of your specific policy.

Often times, you may also purchase property coverage in addition to your primary policy. Property coverage typically covers your liability in the event that a client suffers injury or damage to their personal property while in your office or on your premises.

It is also a good idea to check whether your coverage extends to people other than clients who enter your building, e.g. family members of clients, office employees, a plumber, etc.

Do I Need It?

Whether you are working with clients in any medium, such as in person, on the phone, or via the internet, here is the golden rule:

> IF YOU SEE CLIENTS, YOU NEED PROFESSIONAL LIABILITY INSURANCE.

Never work with a client, not even once, without being covered by professional liability insurance. The risk is just not worth it.

Where Do I Get It?

While you are seeing clients in an agency setting during graduate school and before licensure, it is likely that you will be covered under your fieldwork site's policy.

Be sure to ask, and request a copy of this policy for your records. Personally review this policy to ensure it covers pre-licensed professionals. In California, make sure this coverage includes both MFT Trainees and MFT Interns.

If you are not covered by your workplace, or if you want additional insurance for peace of mind, check with your state licensing board for professional liability insurance company recommendations.

> TIP: MANY INSURANCE COMPANIES OFFER STUDENT LIABILITY INSURANCE PROGRAMS AT A REDUCED RATE.

Chapter 21
Becoming a Registered Intern

You have graduated from your MFT program. Your graduation is a huge milestone in and of itself. Congratulations! You now have a Master's degree.

Take a moment to stop and reflect on how far you have come. Celebrate this accomplishment.

A few years have gone by since you began your MFT journey and, for some, priorities or goals may have shifted. In terms of The Therapy Three, you are one third of the way there.

Gut Check

Assess how you are feeling about your progress and your current path toward MFT licensure.

Do you want to continue on the MFT road?

_____

_____

_____

Is there something else you want to do with your Master's instead of becoming licensed as an MFT?

_____

_____

_____

Do you want to do something else entirely?

_____

_____

_____

Take a moment to consider your options. If you do decide to step off of this path, grant yourself permission to do so without shame or guilt.

The Next Phase

For those of you who want to continue on, welcome to the next phase along the road to MFT licensure.

Take this time to re-check your state licensure requirements.

- Have any of your state licensure requirements changed? If so, alter the charts you made in Chapter 17 accordingly.

- What does your state licensing board require of you after graduation?

- Is there anything you need to mail into your state licensing board?

In California, after you graduate from your MFT program, you must apply for an MFT Intern registration number within 90 days. If you fail to do so, you cannot count the hours you earn during this time toward your licensure requirement. Do not delay applying for your MFT Intern registration number. Plan on mailing your MFT Intern registration application within one week after you graduate.

Your state licensing board receives many of intern registration applications and processing them all takes time. Postponing sending in your application could cost you unnecessary hours.

> TIP: ALWAYS MAKE A COPY OF EVERYTHING YOU
> SEND INTO YOUR STATE LICENSING BOARD, AND GET A
> TRACKING NUMBER.

Once you receive your intern registration number, you have six years to complete your hours. If you take longer, you must apply for a second intern registration number. If you receive a second intern registration number, you will be unable to work in a private practice setting during the period of this second intern registration.

> TIP: DO NOT LET YOUR INTERN REGISTRATION NUMBER
> EXPIRE. MARK THE EXPIRATION DATE ON YOUR CALENDAR
> IN BRIGHT RED.

In most states, any hours accumulated with an expired intern registration will not count toward your licensing requirement. In essence, during the time your registration is expired, you will be working for free and making the road to MFT licensure that much longer. So stay on top of it!

Changing Clinical Sites

This natural transition in your path to MFT licensure is a good time to consider changing clinical sites to vary your clinical experience and training. Once you are licensed, it is more difficult to get a varied clientele, so take advantage of this time.

> TIP: WHEN LEAVING AN INTERNSHIP SITE, PUT A COPY
> OF THE SITE'S CONSENT FORMS IN YOUR FILES TO ASSIST
> YOU IN DRAFTING YOUR OWN FORMS ONCE YOU ARE
> LICENSED.

With whom are you interested in working that you haven't yet?

_____

_____

_____

_____

Does your state have a minimum number of hours that needs to be gained within a particular category? See the charts you completed in Chapter 17 for this information.

Finding A New Clinical Placement

Find out if you can still use your graduate program's resources to find a new internship. If not, here are some resources that may help:

- www.craigslist.com: Search under "Jobs" for counselor, MFTI, MFT, therapist

- Your local professional association's website and/or magazine

- www.alltherapyjobs.com

- www.socialservice.com

With all of the classes, workshops, and hours required as an MFT Intern, it can be tempting to want to act the part. I think that perhaps, once you're licensed, you realize there isn't one. Therapy is a reciprocal relationship, and no two clients will ever be the same. Learn everything you can from your clients and the people around you. Learn everything you can, that is, and then forget it. What you are left with is you. If you've done your own work, that's what most people need: you to be you.

~ Tamara Hostetler, MFT, Private Practice, Former Head Counselor and Coordinator for Marin County Dixie School District, San Francisco

Chapter 22
Pace Yourself

Does it feel like the race is on to get your hours? It can be easy to get hooked into getting as many hours as fast as you can. Be careful, as this approach often leads to burnout.

Many states have a minimum and maximum number of years in which to accumulate hours before applying for licensure. Review the charts you made in Chapter 17, and then take a deep breath. There is time.

It is important to pace yourself for this leg of the journey because this stretch requires the most endurance. These years of training as an MFT Intern can be difficult. It can be daunting, demoralizing, and frustrating to work for free or little pay while you slowly trudge your way through your state board's licensing requirement for collecting hours. You will likely have little say in the types or quantity of clients you have in your caseload, and this section of the MFT road can at times seem never-ending.

Take heart. Remind yourself that this training period is finite. If you choose to enter a private practice upon licensure, you will determine your schedule, your client caseload, your fee, and the way you manage all aspects of your practice. You will be able to choose your clients and can tailor all aspects of your practice to best suit your needs, personality, and lifestyle.

> *Psychotherapy is a demanding vocation, and the successful therapist must be able to tolerate the isolation, anxiety, and frustration that are inevitable in the work.*
> ~ *Irvin Yalom,* The Gift of Therapy

Here are some insider tips to make this part of the process a little quicker, easier, and more enjoyable:

- **Get a mentor.** Though it is easy to feel isolated along the road to licensure, you are not alone! A mentor can help you identify your needs, provide inspiration and encouragement, and help move you toward your goals. A mentor can be paid or unpaid.

Where do you find one? Contact your professional association. In California, CAMFT has a volunteer mentor program that members can access through the CAMFT website.

Other options include hiring a coach or approaching other professionals you know or admire and asking if they are interested in mentoring you.

- **Get your hands on the exam materials.** Similar to my tip when you were still in graduate school, you may again be wondering, "Why would I start studying for my exams now?" Do not worry, I am not suggesting that you start studying for your exams now or that you buy the exam materials at this point because they are very expensive and will probably be updated by the time you are ready to take your exams.

It has, however, been awhile since you were in school and a lot of the material you have studied (and will need to know for the exams) has since evaporated from your overworked and overtired brain cells. Keeping this material fresh will not only help you in your work with your clients but will make studying for the exam a much easier and faster process.

Many newly licensed therapists will donate their exam materials to their internship sites or advertise them online.

- **Remember your self-care.** Do not spread yourself too thin. Remember that part of being a good therapist is taking care of yourself. Make time for yourself by exercising regularly, eating well, seeking the company of supportive friends and family, and getting enough sleep. Take regular breaks away from the therapy world, and give your heart and brain a break. Remember to take advantage of those personal psychotherapy hours!

- **Start networking.** Networking is a big part of getting clients once you are licensed. Most people wait until after they are licensed to start networking. Hint: You do not have to wait!

  Now is a good time to start getting your name known in your community. By developing a professional presence now, you will be one step ahead of your colleagues once you get licensed. Start attending your professional association's local chapter meetings.

  If you need to work while you are getting your hours, why not explore jobs that will complement your current path to licensure? For example, if you want to work with kids in your MFT practice, why not look for a job at a school where you will have the opportunity to network with parents? Once you are licensed, these parents and school personnel will be good referral sources.

See Chapter 41 for more information on networking.

- **Start your marketing efforts now.** Most interns do not have a website or business cards and are not using this valuable time to start getting known in their community. Just as with networking, the time you spend now on marketing can be very valuable once you are licensed and trying to build your business.

> TIP: READ CHAPTERS 39 + 40 ON MARKETING NOW. ALSO SEE APPENDIX E FOR A LIST OF MARKETING RESOURCES.

- **Put your financial needs to work for you.** Many people have a full-time "day job" in addition to their internship. After getting licensed, these people often quit their job to build a private practice. This leap can be a difficult one financially.

One option is to have two part-time jobs plus your internship. Then, after you get licensed, you can quit one of your part-time jobs, thereby allowing yourself to have time to dedicate to your practice while still receiving an income. Even better if that part-time job can be something that will provide referral sources to your practice, as mentioned above.

- **Diversify.** It is easy to get stuck in the mindset of focusing exclusively on getting your hours at this stage. It is important though, at this point, to do things that will build your career in other ways.

  For example: What are your goals post-licensure? If one of them is to teach, start teaching now. You have your Master's degree, so inquire at your local community college or online colleges for full or part-time teaching positions. You might also want to inquire at your local community center or church about conducting a professional seminar or workshop. Be creative, and start diversifying yourself.

- **Make friends in your internship site(s).** Make the effort now, and build your future support system and referral network at the same time. The experience of being a therapist in private practice

can be isolating, so ta**k**
your proximity to fellow **i**
this stage.

- **Remember your support** **.em.**
Make time to see friends outside of the
therapy world to ground yourself and to
get a break. Also, spend time with the
friends you made in graduate school to
help motivate each other through this
leg of the journey.

  There are several online blogs and
  support groups for MFTs en route to
  licensure. Here are a couple worth
  exploring:

  - www.mfthandbook.blogspot.com
  - www.mftinterns.wordpress.com
  - www.mftsfbay.blogspot.com

- **Review:** Now is also a good time to
review the following chapters:

  - Chapter 12: Applying To A
  Fieldwork Site

  - Chapter 18: Personal
  Psychotherapy

  - Chapter 20: Professional Liability

ur Clinical Style

During these training years, take advantage of the opportunity to learn about how you best work. This information will inform your decisions if you choose to set up a private practice upon licensure.

How many clients do you like having in your caseload?

_____

_____

How many clients can you comfortably see in a day?

_____

_____

What time of day are you at your best?

_____

_____

What time of day are you at your worst?

_____

_____

What is the latest appointment you like to schedule?

_____

_____

What helps you not get behind in your notes?

_____

_____

What works best for you in terms of balancing other parts of your life?

_____

_____

TIP: REMEMBER TO ADD YOUR INTERNSHIP EXPERIENCES TO THE JOURNAL YOU STARTED IN CHAPTER 7. LIST YOUR CURRENT CLINICAL STRENGTHS, WEAKNESSES, AND YOUR THOUGHTS ON THE CLINICAL POPULATIONS WITH WHOM YOU'VE WORKED SO FAR. ANY NEW THOUGHTS ON POSSIBLE CLINICAL SPECIALTIES? SEE APPENDIX B FOR A LIST OF SAMPLE NICHES.

Chapter 23
Hours... Complete!

Congratulations! Yet another step forward on your road to licensure. Once again, be sure to celebrate this accomplishment. You made it through the trenches! Get a massage, have a fun night out, go to a spa, dance until you can't breathe, go camping... you get the idea. Just do something special and celebratory to mark this grand achievement.

> TIP: CELEBRATING YOUR ACCOMPLISHMENTS ALONG THE WAY TO LICENSURE CAN PREVENT BURNOUT AND INCREASE YOUR MOTIVATION TO MAKE IT TO THE FINISH LINE.

Now, send in your application for state licensure. You have worked so hard and so long for this day, and yet a lot of people procrastinate taking the next step and sending in their application.

Re-read the MFT practice journal for clues as to what might be coming up for you in your resistance to mailing in your application. Maybe you are scared about what comes next. Perhaps the idea of having to study for the exams seems too overwhelming. Maybe you are not sure that you want to get licensed anymore or have other life situations that need to take priority for now.

Whatever the emotion, let it have center stage so you can fully explore it and make the right decision for yourself. Then, if all systems are go... mail your application.

> TIP: MAKE COPIES OF YOUR COMPLETE APPLICATION, AND REMEMBER TO GET A TRACKING NUMBER.

SECTION FOUR:
Passing the Exams

Chapter 24
Study Materials

You are ready to start studying for the final leg of The Therapy Three... passing your exam(s)! Remember to stay focused and use the motivational and support tools already discussed to keep yourself moving toward the finish line.

> TIP: IF YOUR STATE REQUIRES MORE THAN ONE EXAM FOR LICENSURE, TRY TO TAKE THEM AS CLOSE TOGETHER AS POSSIBLE, PREFERABLY WITHIN A FEW WEEKS. MUCH OF THE MATERIAL YOU STUDY WILL BE THE SAME, SO WHY WAIT AND THEN HAVE TO RE-LEARN IT?

There are two questions I invariably hear:

- "Should I invest in study materials?"

- "If so, from where should I get my study materials?"

Let's look at each question individually.

Should I Invest in Study Materials?

The short answer is: if you can afford it, yes. Although I do know a couple of people who have passed their exams without formal study materials, do you really want to chance it after having worked so hard to get to this point?

In many states, you will have to wait a certain number of months before being able to retake an exam in the event that you do not pass. For California, you must wait six months. Do yourself the favor of being as well prepared as possible to increase your chances of only having to go through the exam process once.

As mentioned in earlier chapters, many newly licensed therapists sell or give away their study materials. If finances are an issue (and they often are after having worked so long for so little), check the following resources for used study materials:

- Craigslist: www.craigslist.com

- Your past fieldwork and internship site(s)

- Friends from graduate school who may now be licensed

- The program manager from your graduate school

Where Should I Buy Materials?

Once you have decided to invest in study materials, the next question is from what company should you purchase the materials? There are several different options.

Although each company offers similar study formats, explore their sample materials online to understand with which you feel most comfortable. Be sure to inquire about each company's money-back guarantees and whether they offer a refund if you do not pass your exam. Some of your choices include:

- Gerry Grossman Seminars
  www.gerrygrossman.com

- AATBS
  www.aatbs.com

- PASS:
  www.passmftexams.com

- Private tutoring

Each company offers various study packages, including options such as seminars, group study workshops, and at-home study materials. The at-home study materials include options such as audio disks, written study materials, written practice exams, and an online test bank of exam questions.

> TIP: WHAT IS YOUR LEARNING STYLE? DO YOU PREFER STUDY GROUPS? DO YOU FIND STUDYING WITH OTHERS TOO DISTRACTING? ARE YOU AN AUDIO OR A VISUAL LEARNER? TO SAVE MONEY ON STUDY MATERIALS, ONLY INVEST IN THE STUDY FORMATS THAT SUPPORT YOUR INDIVIDUAL LEARNING STYLE.

If it is in your budget, purchase or borrow a study package that includes a variety of formats. You never know what will stick!

> TIP: IT IS CRUCIAL TO PRACTICE TAKING THE EXAM IN THE SAME FORMAT AS THE REAL EXAM. IF YOU WILL BE TAKING THE REAL EXAM ON A COMPUTER, INVEST IN ONLINE PRACTICE EXAMS THROUGH THE ONLINE TEST BANKS AVAILABLE FROM THE ABOVE COMPANIES.

Chapter 25
Emotional Preparation

D o not psyche yourself out about the exams. Remember that thousands of individuals before you have taken these exams and, whether they passed on the first time or had to re-take an exam, they survived.

Here are some tips to make preparing for your exam(s) a little easier:

- **Practice What You Preach:** Exercise the self-care that you undoubtedly have encouraged your clients to practice.

- **Pace Yourself:** Aim for getting consistently high scores on your practice exams. Schedule your exam when you feel ready. If you schedule your exam and then do not feel you are ready, reschedule it.

- **Balance:** Do not go overboard on studying. Remember your life, and maintain a balance. There is something to be said for knowing when to take a break.

- **Support system:** Do not exist in a vacuum. Let your family, friends, and colleagues know that you are studying so that they can be supportive and help to motivate and encourage you. At the same time, do not feel pressured to tell anyone the exact date of your scheduled exam. For some, this information may cause too much pressure.

- **Prepare for Re-taking the Exam:** It is okay if you do not pass the first time. Many don't. Let yourself off this hook now, and your studying efforts will benefit.

  Also, let your support system know that many do not pass these exams on the first try to manage expectations and to release the pressure valve a little. Not passing the first time is neither a sign of being a bad therapist nor a sign of intelligence.

Do your best, and that is all you can do.

Chapter 26
How To Study

Plan to study for an average of three months for your first exam. If you have more than one licensing exam, aim to take the second exam within one month of passing the first exam.

During these twelve weeks of studying for your first exam, it is important to follow a formal written study guide. This plan may be included in the study materials you have purchased. If not, devise your own.

If making your own study guide, write down a list of general topics you need to study, as defined by your state licensing board. Divide these topics into sections according to your study materials and available formats. Assign these topics to a twelve-week calendar. Check the sections off as you go to mark your progress.

There is a vast amount of material to study, and it can get overwhelming. In general, it can be helpful to follow these general guidelines while studying:

1. Read through a section of the written material.

2. Listen to the corresponding audio CD.

3. Go to the online bank of study questions and practice what you have just studied.

For example, if you just finished reading about law and ethics, listen to the audio CD about law and ethics the next time you are in your car to reinforce the concepts. When you get home, use the online test bank to take some practice questions about law and ethics. Studying in various formats, one section at a time, will help to reinforce the material.

At the end of this chapter, you will find a sample study guide using California's content areas. This sample study guide assumes a study package that includes a reading manual, CD's, flashcards, and twelve online practice exams. Adjust this guide to match your study package.

Note that this sample study guide includes taking a timed practice exam at the end of your first week of studying to get your baseline score. Expect your baseline score to be low since you are at the beginning of your studies.

After getting your baseline score, continue taking practice exams each week but do not time yourself. Just get accustomed to the format. Once you are comfortable with the exam format and have been studying for a while, start timing yourself during the exams so you can begin to pace yourself for the real exam.

Go through the entire sequence of practice exams in order, taking each exam once. Then once you are finished with all of the practice exams, begin again with the first exam. Aim to go through the series of practice exams at least twice.

By the time you are going through the series of practice exams a second time, your scores should be increasing by roughly 20%. Record your scores on the chart at the end of this chapter so that you can monitor your progress.

> TIP: DO NOT GET OVERLY DISCOURAGED BY A SCORE ON ANY SINGLE PRACTICE EXAM.

If you are not seeing a 20% improvement on your second round of practice exams versus your first round, do not panic. Continue to review your materials, identify your weaknesses, and consider joining a study group or attending a live workshop.

Inquire with your internship site, your state licensing board, or your local professional organization about existing study groups. Some study groups also advertise online.

You are in the last stretch here, so stick to it.

SAMPLE STUDY GUIDE

Wk	Reading (Section)	CD's	Flash-cards	Practice Exams
1	Law & Ethics	CD #1		Exam #1 (timed) =Baseline
2	Law & Ethics	CD #1	Yes	Exam #2 (untimed)
3	Clinical Evaluation	CD #2		Exam #3 (untimed)
4	Clinical Evaluation	CD #2	Yes	Exams #4+5 (untimed)
5	Crisis Management	CD #3+4	Yes	Exams #6+7 (start timing)
6	Treatment	CD #5		Exam #8+9
7	Treatment	CD#6	Yes	Exam #10+11
8	Treatment Planning	Review CD #1+2		Exams #12+1
9	Treatment Planning	Review CD #3+4	Yes	Exams #2-3
10	Review Weak Areas	Review CD #5+6	Review	Exams #4-6
11	Review All	Review all	Review	Exams #7-9
12	Review All	Review all	Review	Exams #10-12

PRACTICE EXAM SCORES

Exam	Timed/Untimed	Score 1st Round	2nd Round
1	Timed =Baseline		
2	Untimed		
3	Untimed		
4	Untimed		
5	Untimed		
6	Timed		
7	Timed		
8	Timed		
9	Timed		
10	Timed		
11	Timed		
12	Timed		

Chapter 27
Scheduling Your Exams

W hen you have scored consistently high on your practice exams and feel ready, take the plunge and schedule your exam.

> TIP: SET YOURSELF UP FOR SUCCESS WHEN SCHEDULING YOUR EXAMS.

Not a morning person? Try not to schedule your exam first thing in the morning. Many testing sites offer later starting times on certain days. Some sites also offer weekend scheduling.

Questions To Ask

When you schedule your exam date and time, here are some things to ask:

- Can I bring food and/or water into the testing room? If not, will I have access to food and/or water during exam breaks?

- How many breaks are allowed?

- Will the exam timer continue while I am on a break?

- Will scratch paper be available during the exam?

- What do I need to bring for the exam in terms of identification?

- If I need to cancel my exam date, what is the procedure for rescheduling?

- How far in advance do I need to cancel?

- How soon can I reschedule?

Directions

Get the exact address of the testing site, and print out detailed directions.

- Google Maps: maps.google.com

- MapQuest: www.mapquest.com

> TIP: IF POSSIBLE, TAKE A PRACTICE DRIVE TO YOUR TESTING SITE SO YOU DO NOT HAVE ANY UNEXPECTED SURPRISES ON THE DAY OF YOUR EXAM.

Chapter 28
Taking Your Exams

As the day of your exam approaches, practice your self-care by getting enough sleep, exercising, eating well, seeking the company of supportive people, taking quiet time for yourself, and having some fun.

Night Before the Exam

Take care of the practical necessities. You do not want to have to think about anything else on the day of the exam except staying calm and getting to the testing center on time.

Put together a bag with everything you will need on the day of the exam so it is ready to go. Whether or not you can bring these items into the exam room, you will still want them in your car before and after your exam.

Pack bottled water, some energy bars, a banana, lip moisturizer, and your directions to the testing center. Lay out what you are going to wear. Charge your cell phone. Make sure you have enough gas in your car.

> TIP: PLAN TO WEAR COMFORTABLE CLOTHES FOR YOUR EXAM(S), AND BRING LAYERS SINCE THE EXAM ROOM MIGHT BE WARM OR COOL. YOU MAY NOT BE ABLE TO WEAR A JACKET INTO THE EXAM ROOM, SO PLAN ACCORDINGLY.

Do not study or take a practice exam the night before the exam. You will not learn anything new, and you will only increase your anxiety. Instead, do something fun. Go out with friends for an early dinner, see an early movie, or read a light-hearted book. Do not drink alcohol the night before your exam.

Go to bed early. Set two alarms for backup, allowing yourself plenty of time the next morning to get ready without rushing. If necessary, take a mild sleep aid to ease anxiety and to help you sleep.

> TIP: IF YOU TAKE A SLEEP AID, MAKE SURE THAT IT IS SOMETHING YOU HAVE TAKEN BEFORE AND DOES NOT LEAVE YOU FEELING GROGGY IN THE MORNING. IF IN DOUBT, DO NOT TAKE IT.

Day of the Exam

Look in the mirror, and tell yourself the following affirmations:

- I have worked hard to get to this point, and I am proud of myself.

- My self-worth is not determined by this exam.

- If I do not pass, I can take it again.

- I will do my best, and that is all I can do.

- I am ready!

During the Exam

Breathe. If there is something you do not know, mark the question so you can return to it and move on. Do not let a single question derail you. Repeat the above affirmations if anxiety strikes.

Remember to take breaks. Prevent getting tired by taking a quick bathroom break. Do some stretching. If allowed, drink water and eat a snack to keep up your energy. If no food is allowed during the exams, splash your face with cold water in the bathroom to wake yourself up and keep your mind fresh.

Watch the clock, and remember to pace yourself.

Chapter 29
Exam Results

If you did not pass, you are not a failure. Take the time to grieve the result, scream into a pillow, cry, swear at the insanity of standardized tests, and get some sleep. Take care of yourself while you reassess your next step.

My suggestion is to realize that many people do not pass on the first try and to get back on the horse. Study some more, consider different study materials, enlist the aid of your support system, and take it again. You can do it!

If you did pass, please proceed to the next section.

SECTION FIVE:
You've Made It! Now What?

Chapter 30
Celebrate!

Congratulations! You passed your exam(s). The congratulating is not over, but here are a couple of quick tips before you go on your vacation or put all things MFT out of your mind for a little while.

> TIP: DO NOT THROW OUT YOUR STUDY MATERIALS.

Although you may have the urge to throw away all of your study materials as a gesture of having made it, don't! You might want to refer to them when you are practicing, sell them, or donate them to someone else just beginning their journey.

> TIP: COMPLETE ANY NECESSARY PAPERWORK NOW TO RECEIVE YOUR LICENSE.

Is there any other paperwork you need to complete to receive your license? If so, get this done right away since your state licensing board can get backed up. You do not want any delays in receiving your license.

Now again...

CONGRATULATIONS!

CELEBRATE!

Chapter 31
Now What?

You have your MFT license. You are official. How does it feel? Now that you have had time to revel in your huge accomplishment of having traversed The Therapy Three successfully, take the time to reflect once again on the following questions:

- What are your goals at this point?

- Have your goals changed since you started the MFT road?

- What do you want to do with your license?

- Do you still want to be a therapist?

- What is your next step?

- Do you want to start a private practice?

- Do you want to enter a group practice?

- Would you prefer to work at an agency?

- Do you want to do a mix of both agency and private practice?

- Do you want your practice to be a hobby or a business?

- What will be your niche, your area of clinical specialty?

- What is your overall vision for your career?

> TIP: REVIEW THE MFT JOURNAL THAT YOU BEGAN IN CHAPTER 7 FOR NICHE IDEAS. SEE APPENDIX B FOR A LIST OF SAMPLE NICHES.

Your MFT License

Many of you may already know what you want to do with your license, while others may not. Your hard-earned license can be put to work in many different ways. Some will choose the route of opening a private practice.

What are some other options? Here are some ideas. Get creative, and make your career work for you.

- Inpatient hospital staff

- Human resources personnel

- College admissions counselor

- Writer

- Mediator

- Life coach

- Researcher

- Director of a non-profit organization

- Administrative role in a community mental health agency

- Supervisory role in a community mental health agency

- Organizational consultant

- Public policy researcher

- Television talk show host

- Teacher (A college professor usually has a doctorate degree. For Masters level MFTs, first explore local community or online colleges.)

- School Psychologist (requires additional training)

- School Counselor

- Employee Assistance Program (EAP) staff

- Health Maintenance Organization (HMO) staff

- Other: _____

- Other: _____

- Other: _____

Chapter 32
Traits For Success

If your career goals include starting a private practice, consider the following attributes common to successful small business owners:

- They persistently look for solutions to problems.

- They are optimistic when facing a problem.

- They persevere by maintaining their vision of their business.

- They are aware of the bottom line and seek profit.

- They work hard.

- They have strong organizational skills.

Take a moment to assess your current strengths and growth areas as they relate to the above attributes. Consider the following questions:

Which of the above attributes are current strengths of yours?

_____

_____

_____

_____

_____

How do you currently exhibit these attributes in your daily life?

_____

_____

_____

_____

_____

Upon which of these attributes could you improve?

_____

_____

_____

_____

_____

_____

How are you going to make these improvements, and what is your timeline for these improvements?

_____

_____

_____

_____

_____

Why do you want to enter private practice?

_____

_____

_____

_____

_____

What are your fears around entering private practice?

_____

_____

_____

_____

_____

The following chapters will apply primarily to those who choose the route of opening a private practice.

Chapter 33
Private Practice

You have decided to start a private practice. Congratulations! This decision marks the end goal for many people who begin the MFT journey.

> *"If we all did the things we are capable of doing, we would literally astound ourselves."*
> ~ Thomas Edison

What does your ideal private practice look like? Return to your MFT journal for inspiration and guidance. You have learned a lot about yourself and your style of practicing in the past few years. Now it is time to tailor your preferences into a practice that works for you.

Write down your vision of your ideal practice. Be specific.

How many clients do you have?

_____

_____

What types of clients do you see?

_____

_____

What is your weekly schedule?

_____

_____

How many weeks per year do you work?

_____

_____

What is your hourly fee for individuals, couples, families, and groups?

_____

_____

Are you in a group practice, or a solo practice?

_____

_____

Are you on insurance panels?

_____

_____

Do you only accept private pay clients?

_____

_____

Do you have a sliding scale?

_____

_____

What are your monthly and yearly gross and net incomes?

_____

_____

Where is your office located?

_____

_____

Do you share an office, or do you have your own?

_____

_____

Are you on the lease, or are you subleasing?

_____

_____

How is your office and waiting room decorated?

_____

_____

How do you manage your billing and client records?

_____

_____

How and when do you take client notes?

_____

_____

How do you manage your calendar?

_____

_____

How do you market yourself?

_____

_____

What types of professional associations are you a part of, and what role do you have in these associations?

_____

_____

_____

Are there other aspects to your practice, such as giving workshops or seminars?

_____

_____

_____

_____

Where do you want your practice to be in one year? Five years? Ten?

_____

_____

_____

_____

Take a moment to think about your career goals. Do you want your practice to be the mainstay of your career, or will your practice be only one part of your professional identity? Do you also want to teach, write, or consult? What is your timeline for wanting to incorporate these other avenues?

By having a vision of where you want to go, you will be best prepared to get there. There are many things you can do with your license; you are only limited by your imagination!

The journey from licensing to private practice can feel very exciting and yet incredibly lonely. I found this to be a difficult transition that was made smoother when I sought out my own support, built my own community and, most importantly, learned to tolerate the anxiety that came with realizing my dream. It was most helpful to remind myself, after completing all of the necessary steps to finally reach this destination, that I would not be here unless I was meant to be here. I still do this!
~ Melyssa Nelson, MFT, Private Practice,
San Francisco

Chapter 34
Your Practice Niche

One of the best things you can do to succeed in private practice is to develop a practice niche for your business. A practice niche is equivalent to a clinical specialty.

The Generalist

There are thousands of licensed MFTs in private practice, and a good portion of them are generalists. A generalist is someone who does not specialize in a certain population or problem. A drawback to the generalist approach is that there is little to set you apart from the masses of other therapists. Without a niche, you may appear to be good at many things but a master of none.

Put yourself in the role of a client while reflecting on the following scenarios:

1. You are looking for a therapist for your 12-year-old son who is being bullied at school.

   Which of the following therapists would you call for an appointment?

   a) A therapist who specializes in working with adolescent victims and perpetrators of bullying.

   b) A therapist who sees children who are being bullied, as well as couples dealing with infidelity, children struggling with death, men who are lacking a relationship, and women who are anxious.

2. You are married and are looking for a couples counselor to improve the communication in your marriage.

   Which of the following therapists would you call for an appointment?

   a) A therapist who specializes in working with couples and communication.

   b) A therapist who works with couples who are fighting a lot, as well as toddlers with ADHD, women with a terminal illness, couples who have decided to divorce, and CEO's who lack a relationship.

As you can see from the above scenarios, a niche will set you apart from the masses and give your clients confidence that you are an expert in their problem.

> TIP: YOUR GOAL IS TO BECOME KNOWN AS AN EXPERT IN YOUR NICHE.

Your Ideal Client

Who is your ideal client? Think about *who* you want to work with and on *what* clinical issues. This combination defines your ideal client and the niche to whom you should market.

Keep in mind that the best niches are the most focused in terms of the following:

1. Population (who)

2. Problem (what)

In reviewing your MFT journal, with whom do you like working the most? Just as importantly, with whom do you not want to work? It can be helpful to think about past clients you have had and what you liked or did not like about working with them.

Remember that your practice niche must be marketable. Your ideal client must also be able to afford your services.

> TIP: THINK ABOUT WHAT YOUR IDEAL CLIENTS WORRY ABOUT IN THE MIDDLE OF THE NIGHT. WHAT WOULD LEAD THEM TO SPEND THEIR HARD-EARNED MONEY TO SEE YOU?

Discovering Your Niche

In defining your practice niche, it can be helpful to think about the different niche markets to which you belong. Describing yourself in these terms can help elucidate the potential niche markets you may want to serve.

To what populations do you belong? Some examples might be married, raised Catholic, only child, dentist, antique phonograph collector, and English as a second language.

What problems have you experienced? Some examples might be cancer, infertility, divorce, insomnia, and anxiety.

Complete the chart below, and be as specific as you can.

Populations To Which I Belong	Problems I Have Experienced

Next, complete the following charts for populations and problems you may or may not want to serve, and be as specific as possible. These charts will assist you in defining your ideal client and to whom your marketing efforts will target.

Populations With Who I Am Interested In Working	Populations With Whom I Do Not Want To Work

Problems in which I am interested	Problems in which I am not interested

Now combine the populations and problems in which you are interested, and see what sparks.

Following are some examples:

Niche: Aggressive adolescent boys
Who: Adolescent boys
What: Aggressive behavior

Niche: Single women who want a relationship
Who: Single women
What: Lack of a relationship

Niche: Fathers who have lost a child
Who: Fathers
What: The loss of a child (grief and loss)

Niche: Couples trying to recover from an affair
Who: Couples
What: Infidelity

Niche: Mothers of the bride who are having relationship problems with their daughters
Who: Mothers of the bride
What: Relationship problems with bride

Niche: Recently divorced men
Who: Men
What: Recently divorced

TIP: PUT THE PROBLEM INTO THE CLIENT'S LANGUAGE.
DO NOT USE CLINICAL TERMS.

Niche: _____

Who: _____

What: _____

Niche: _____

Who: _____

What: _____

Niche: _____

Who: _____

What: _____

Niche: _____

Who: _____

What: _____

TIP: SEE APPENDIX B FOR A SAMPLE LIST OF ADDITIONAL NICHES.

Chapter 35
The Business of Therapy

A private practice is a small business. Most therapists are right-brained creatures by nature and tend to experience brain freeze when the practical and left-brained matters of running a small business come into play.

Do not fret. You are not alone, and you *can* be successful with the business end of running a private practice.

The first thing you need to do is to develop a business plan that takes into consideration your budget, expenses, and specific short-term and long-term financial goals. This plan does not need to be a 100-page PowerPoint presentation, but it does need to be well thought out.

Begin by charting your expenses below.

Expenses	Cost	Schedule (monthly/yearly)
Rent (include cleaning)		
CEUs		
Stationary		
Professional Associations		
Insurance		
Telephone		
Voicemail		
Furniture		
Calendar		
Office Supplies		
Fax Machine		
Computer		
Filing Cabinet		
Magazines (for waiting room)		
Administration		
Parking		
Trainings		
MFT License Fee		
Personal Therapy		
Supervision		
Marketing		
Other		
TOTAL		

You will use the data from this chart to create your business plan.

Business Plan

> TIP: IN DEVELOPING YOUR BUSINESS PLAN, THINK ABOUT WHAT YOU NEED TO EARN PER WEEK TO MEET YOUR YEARLY FINANCIAL GOALS. HOW MUCH DO YOU NEED TO CHARGE PER SESSION TO MEET YOUR WEEKLY GOALS? HOW MANY CLIENTS DO YOU NEED? PLAY WITH THE NUMBERS TO FIND A COMBINATION THAT WORKS FOR YOU. REMEMBER TO FACTOR IN YOUR ANNUAL VACATIONS.

Refer to the U.S. Small Business Administration's website for a business plan outline and other helpful tools to assist you in running your small business.

- www.sba.gov/smallbusinessplanner/index.html

Naming Your Business

What will you name your business? Most therapists in private practice are sole proprietors and use their legal name as their practice name. Others choose to use a fictitious business name. If you choose the latter, you will need to file a "DBA," or "doing business as" with your county.

EIN

Get yourself a Tax Identification Number, also called an Employer Identification Number or EIN. You will need this EIN to set up a business bank account. Having an EIN will also minimize your need to give out your social security number unnecessarily, which is always a good idea with the increase of identify theft cases. You may apply for and receive your EIN online at the IRS website:

- www.irs.gov/business/small

Bank Account and Credit Card

Set up a business checking account, and get a business credit card. Using your business credit card only for business expenses will go a long way to making tax time that much easier.

Taxes

For more information on taxes, please see Chapter 36.

Retirement

It can seem odd to be thinking about retirement when you are just starting a practice, but it is vital to do so. Being self-employed, you are in charge of creating your retirement funds. Inquire with your bank now about setting up an IRA.

Client Fees

Will you take insurance, or will you only accept private pay clients? This decision will greatly impact your business, so be sure to explore your options. As with many aspects of setting up your practice, there is no right or wrong answer. The right choice for you depends on your financial situation, your tolerance for paperwork, your ideal client load, and the client population you wish to see.

If you decide to accept insurance, you must join an insurance panel(s). Ask trusted colleagues for their opinions and experiences with their insurance panels. Make an informed decision on which panels to join, and be sure to read the fine print to understand what your contract requires before signing anything.

Billing

For billing and practice management solutions, please see Chapter 37.

Know your worth. Know that everyone has money issues, both therapists and clients. The more you explore this area on your own, the more depth your practice will have. Most importantly, you will know when to say "no" and refer out those who aren't within either your scope of practice or competence. Building a healthy, sustaining practice takes time. When I didn't need clients, they came. If you need to balance your life with another job until you can sustain a practice full-time, then do it. Do not overly commit and, thereby, take on clients who really don't fit your style.

~ Tamara Hostetler, MFT, Private Practice, Former Head Counselor & Coordinator for Marin County Dixie School District, San Francisco

Chapter 36
Taxes, Part II

Note: The information in this chapter does not represent tax advice and should not be assumed to be free of errors. When in doubt, contact the IRS, a tax accountant, or an income tax service.

I am not a tax expert and, chances are, neither are you. So *before* tax time, be sure to educate yourself on exactly what you will be able to deduct so that you can plan ahead.

It is a good idea to talk with a tax accountant or a tax expert to understand exactly how you should keep your records. It is best to understand the laws now, at the beginning of your practice, so the IRS does not come knocking on your door later.

Generally, a certain percentage of the following can be deducted. Make sure to keep all of your receipts and, as with your client records, document, document, document.

> TIP: BE SURE TO CHECK WITH YOUR ACCOUNTANT OR A TAX EXPERT, OR DO YOUR OWN RESEARCH, TO ENSURE THAT YOU ARE TAKING FULL ADVANTAGE OF AVAILABLE DEDUCTIONS!

Possible Deductions

- Home office (defined as being a space devoted solely to your business)

- Office supplies

- Office furniture

- Office equipment

- Software and subscriptions

- Mileage (keep a log in your car and record the date, mileage, tolls, parking costs, etc.)

- Travel, meals, entertainment

- Insurance

- Retirement contribution

- Social Security

- Telephone charges

Quarterly Estimates

If you are self-employed, such as being in private practice, you will most likely be required to pay quarterly estimates since withholding is not being deducted from your income. Your first year in business is usually an exception, since you do not know what your annual gross income will be. Thereafter, you will need to prepare financially for these quarterly payments.

> TIP: IF YOU FAIL TO PAY THE ESTIMATES ON TIME, YOU WILL BE ASSESSED INTEREST AND A PENALTY FINE.

While TurboTax (www.turbotax.com) has a helpful version for small businesses, my best advice is to form a trusting relationship with an accountant who can best guide you through the IRS maze. Mistakes can be costly, so invest in this step of your business.

How do you find an accountant that has experience working with private practice therapists? Ask trusted colleagues for their recommendations. Be sure to comparison shop, as accountants can vary widely on fees.

Chapter 37
Practice Management

There are many choices on how to manage the large amount of paperwork involved in today's psychotherapy private practice. Set yourself up for success by deciding now exactly how you will manage this important aspect of your practice.

A list of all resources mentioned in this chapter can be found in Appendix E.

Practice Forms

Now is the time to put together the practice forms you will be using in your practice. Depending on your state requirements and your niche, you will most likely need the following:

- Adult Client Consent Form

- Minor Client Consent Form

- Client Information/History Form

- Credit Card Pre-Authorization Form (see below)

- Caregiver's Authorization Affidavit

- No Harm/Suicide Contract

- No Secrets Policy

- Authorization to Release Confidential Information

- Group Confidentiality Form

- Client Progress Notes Form

- Treatment Plan Form

- Client Termination Form

- Payment Receipt

- Superbill

- Therapist's Weekly Log

Note that if you are required to be HIPAA compliant, there are additional forms that you will be required to keep. Please contact your state board or state professional association for an explanation of these requirements.

It can save both you and your client time by putting your intake paperwork on your website. When you are making an intake appointment, you can direct your clients to download the intake paperwork, complete it at home, and bring it to the first session. This way, you and your client do not need to spend a good part of the first session doing paperwork.

Templates for each of the above forms can be found in the suggested practice resources listed in Appendix F.

Practice Management Systems

You may keep a paper office, meaning you will keep hard copies of your case files and manage your accounting records separately. If you choose this route, QuickBooks accounting software is a great tool to help you manage your financial records.

- QuickBooks
  www.QuickBooks.com

There are also several practice management software systems on the market. These offer a complete office management system, including full billing and note-taking solutions for today's private practice.

While a discussion of HIPAA is outside the scope of this book, many of the following software packages are also HIPAA compliant.

- Argonaut Software:
  www.argonautsoftware.com

- Therapist Helper
  www.helper.com

- Notes 444
  www.notes444.com

- QuicDoc
  www.quicdoc.com

- Practice Magic
  www.practicemagic.com

Client Payment Policy

A note about fee collection: Accept credit cards! Your clients will appreciate the convenience, and your business will benefit as you minimize payment hassles, such as the forgotten checkbook.

Many therapists are now including a credit card pre-authorization form in their intake paperwork that states that the therapist is authorized to charge the client's credit card for no-shows, late cancellations, and returned check fees.

If you choose to use such a form, get a signed imprint of the client's credit card to minimize any disputes. Portable imprinters are inexpensive and easy to use, although using the side of a pencil on a sales slip can work just as well.

- www.portaprint.com

It is easy to begin accepting credit cards. You do not need a computer or credit card swiper in your office. You can call in the credit card for immediate authorization using your cell phone, or you can input your charges online at the end of the day from the convenience of your own home. You can arrange to have the funds deposited directly into your bank account.

The following resources can help:

- www.propay.com

- www.professionalcharges.com

- www.paypal.com

Chapter 38
Your Office Space

There are many considerations when choosing your office. This process is exciting and offers an opportunity to finally impart some of your taste and aesthetic to your place of business after years of squatting in temporary spaces.

> TIP: THERE IS NO RIGHT OR WRONG WHEN IT COMES TO DECORATING YOUR OFFICE.

What is important to you to have in your office? Before thinking about budget constraints, let yourself dream a little.

Your Ideal Office

What is your ideal office space? How does it look, smell, and sound? Where is it? Think with all of your senses. How do you want to feel walking into your office? How do you want your clients to feel? Is there a waiting room? How does it look, feel, and sound?

My ideal office description:

_____

_____

_____

_____

_____

_____

> TIP: THINK ABOUT THE OFFICES YOU HAVE SEEN DURING YOUR PERSONAL PSYCHOTHERAPY AND SUPERVISION EXPERIENCES. WHAT DID YOU LIKE OR DISLIKE ABOUT THESE SPACES?

Your "Right Now" Office

Revise your ideal office description into a list of priorities. What is most important for you in your first office?

Some considerations may include:

• Price

- Location

- Parking

- Square footage

- Solo practice vs. group practice

- Sharing an office vs. having your own office

- Renting vs. owning

- Length of lease

- Hours/days of availability

- Appearance of building

- Professions of other office occupants

- Level of interaction with other office occupants

- Access to freeway

- Call light system

- Waiting room

- Office lighting

- Design theme

- Colors palette

- Furnishings

- Tea service for clients

- View from office

- Kitchen use

- Soundproofing

- Cleaning service

- Elevator in building

- Other: _____

- Other: _____

- Other: _____

- Other: _____

My "right now" office description:

_____

_____

_____

_____

_____

Finding Your Office

Get a feel for what is available in your area, and consider what fits your budget and needs.

> TIP: TAKE THE TIME TO CHOOSE AN OFFICE THAT REFLECTS WHO YOU ARE AND HOW YOU WANT TO PRACTICE.

Following are two resources to assist you in your search:

- www.craigslist.com
  Search under "Housing/Office and Commercial" for "psychotherapist" or "psychotherapy."

- www.psychoffice.net

> TIP: VISIT SEVERAL OFFICES BEFORE SIGNING A LEASE. IF SUBLEASING, GET EVERYTHING IN WRITING AND ASK FOR A COPY OF THE MASTER LEASE FOR YOUR RECORDS.

Office Decor

As you have heard before, there is no right or wrong when it comes to decorating your office. What is important is that you feel comfortable in your space, that it reflects who you are as a practitioner, and that it is practical for the client population with whom you work.

> TIP: MANY NEWLY LICENSED THERAPISTS SUBLEASE
> THEIR FIRST OFFICE. ASK IF YOU CAN HANG A PIECE OF
> ART, ADD A FEW PILLOWS, OR HAVE A SHELF SO THAT
> YOU ARE REPRESENTED IN THE OFFICE. REMEMBER TO
> ALSO HANG YOUR LICENSE.

Items you might want in your office include:

- Ergonomic therapist's chair
- Couch
- Chair(s)
- Locking filing cabinet
- Desk
- Lamps
- Bookshelf
- Small clocks (one that the client can see, and one that you can see)
- Blanket
- Coffee table
- Rug
- Art

- Mini refrigerator

- Therapy books

- Art materials

- Materials specific to your population, e.g. play therapy equipment

> A WORD ABOUT SAFETY: DO NOT PLACE YOUR THERAPIST'S CHAIR BETWEEN THE DOOR AND WHERE YOUR CLIENT(S) WILL SIT.

Clients who feel threatened or who are threatening can escalate their reactivity if they feel blocked from escape or trapped. Make sure that both you and your client have easy access to the door at all times in case of emergencies. Many therapists also keep their cell phone within reach should an emergency arise.

Chapter 39
Brand Yourself

Your brand is your marketing identity and will consist of your logo, website, and stationary package. When someone sees your brand, you want her/him to think of you and your business.

Most therapists are not designers, so do not fear. There are plenty of resources out there to get you up and running and looking professional. Following are some good places to start.

A list of all resources mentioned in this chapter can be found in Appendix E.

TIP: VISIT THE LINKS PAGE AT WWW.MFTHANDBOOK.COM FOR EXCLUSIVE DISCOUNTS ON MANY OF THE FOLLOWING RESOURCES.

Logo

Your logo will be on your website, business cards, and stationary. You will want a logo that embodies either who you are as a therapist or how you want your clients to feel. Think about what colors are important to you. Sketch or put into words any ideas that you have, then hire a designer to bring it to life.

> TIP: CHOOSE A LOGO THAT WILL ALSO LOOK GOOD WHEN PRINTED IN BLACK AND WHITE, AS COLOR PRINTING CAN BE EXPENSIVE.

For the following resources, you name your budget, describe your idea and needs, and post a contest to a community of talented designers who will bid on your project. Some will even create mock-ups so you can see their designs before you pick a winner. Visit individual websites for program specifics.

- www.99designs.com

- www.elogocontest.com

- www.gfxcontests.com

- www.guru.com

- www.elance.com

Website

Consider a website mandatory for a successful private practice. In today's world, the internet is a powerful source of marketing and has all but replaced the need for a traditional yellow pages ad.

Many clients find a therapist via the internet, yet it is astounding how many therapists do not have a website. Stay one step ahead in this competitive field by getting a web presence. A one-page site is fine. It does not need to be extensive, but it does need to look professional. You can either design your website yourself or hire a web designer.

> TIP: IF YOU ARE NEITHER CREATIVE NOR TECHNICAL, CONSIDER HIRING A WEBSITE DESIGNER. YOUR WEBSITE IS YOUR PROFESSIONAL FACE TO THE WORLD. MAKE IT SHINE!

Self-designed website using a pre-formatted template:

Designing your own website is more cost-effective and a good choice if you are creatively inclined.

- www.homestead.com
  Template-based, well priced, does not offer as many customization options as other services.

- www.godaddy.com
  Template-based and well priced. Site
  can be confusing, and some creative
  experience is necessary.

TIP: FOR A CUSTOMIZED WEBSITE WITH MINIMAL
FINANCIAL OUTPUT AND MAXIMUM IMPACT, I OFFER A
WEBSITE DESIGN PACKAGE USING THIS SOFTWARE THAT IS
EASY TO MAINTAIN YOURSELF.

- www.ForTherapists.com
  Easy to build, template-based websites
  with great hands-on technical support
  for those who need some hand-holding.

- www.webpowertools.com
  Pre-formatted, fully customizable
  websites for those who want more
  creative control. No technical expertise
  needed. Formerly associated with
  EasyTherapySites.com.

- www.TherapySites.com
  A turnkey solution for those that want
  all of the goodies with little effort and
  are willing to pay a higher monthly fee.
  Well-designed, expensive, and currently
  does not offer as many customization
  options as other services.

TIP: NEGOTIATE YOUR PRICE. JUST BECAUSE A CERTAIN PRICE IS ADVERTISED DOES NOT MEAN YOU CANNOT GET A LOWER PRICE. ASK FOR DISCOUNTED RATES.

Hire a website designer:

This option is usually pricier than the above choices since a website is designed just for you. No templates are used, so your site will be 100% unique.

- www.TherapistWebsites.com
  A custom website will be designed just for you.

For the following website resources, you name your budget, describe your idea and needs, and post a contest to a community of talented designers who will bid on your project. Some will even create mock-ups so you can see their designs before you pick a winner. Visit individual websites for program specifics.

- www.guru.com

- www.elance.com

- www.99designs.com

> TIP: WHEN CHOOSING YOUR DOMAIN NAME, BUY A
> DOMAIN ENDING IN ".COM" AND CHOOSE A SHORT NAME
> THAT IS EASY TO SAY AND SPELL. TO BE WELL-RANKED
> IN SEARCH ENGINES, IT IS HELPFUL TO INCLUDE THE
> GEOGRAPHICAL AREA IN YOUR DOMAIN NAME, SUCH AS
> WWW.MARINCOUNTYCOUNSELING.COM

Stationary Package

Your stationary package will consist of the following items:

- Practice announcement (see Appendix D for an example)

- Business cards

- Letterhead

- Envelopes

- Brochure(s)

The following resources can help you with your stationary package:

- www.99designs.com

- www.vistaprint.com

- www.overnightprints.com

- www.printplace.com

TIP: REMEMBER TO VISIT THE LINKS PAGE AT WWW.MFTHANDBOOK.COM FOR DISCOUNTS ON MANY OF THE RESOURCES MENTIONED.

Chapter 40
Marketing 101

A lthough a thorough exploration of marketing is outside the scope of this book, the main avenues to successfully marketing a private practice will be discussed.

Now that you have a website and a brand, it is time to let the public know about you and your practice. Remember that it does not matter how beautiful or professional your materials are if no one is going to see them.

Many therapists shudder when hearing the term "marketing." Some believe any type of sales pitch around their practice to be unprofessional, while others develop dry mouth at the mere thought of public speaking. Others believe that their professional skills and having a website will be enough to bring clients to their door.

Times have changed since the days when word-of-mouth marketing was regularly sufficient to fill a practice. To achieve a successful practice in today's saturated markets, some type of consistent marketing is necessary.

> TIP: THE TRICK TO MARKETING IS TO PICK THE MARKETING METHODS THAT FIT WHO YOU ARE AS A PERSON AND PRACTITIONER.

In the camp of dry mouths when it comes to public speaking? Then don't do it. There is no reason to suffer while marketing your practice. There are many marketing options available to you.

> TIP: YOU WILL BE THE MOST SUCCESSFUL IN YOUR MARKETING EFFORTS IF YOU CHOOSE THOSE OPTIONS THAT YOU ENJOY AND WILL REPEAT.

A list of all resources mentioned in this chapter can be found in Appendix E.

Advertise Your Practice Locally

- Put your brochures on the bulletin boards of local coffee houses, supermarkets, and community centers (always ask permission first).

- Approach complementary practitioners (see the list of potential referral sources below), and ask if you may place your brochures and/or business cards in their waiting rooms.

Advertise Your Practice Online

- List your website for free on all of the major search engines (Google, Yahoo, MSN, etc.).

- Potential clients will often use the internet to find you. There are many online sites where you can list your practice information. There are both free and paid options. Some examples include:

> www.find-a-therapist.com
> www.goodtherapy.org
> www.psychologytoday.com
> www.counsel-search.com
> www.networktherapy.com
> www.theramatch.com
> www.yellowpages.com
> www.4therapy.com
> www.insiderpages.com
> www.wellness.com
> www.everytherapist.com
> www.counselingbook.com

Certain sites are more popular in different regions of the country. You will want to target your listings on the sites most frequented in your area. To find which are most popular in your area, do a sample search online. Type in "therapist" or "MFT" or your specific niche terms into a search engine, plus your city. Note which sites come up on the first couple of pages. These are the sites to target.

> *I would suggest getting yourself on therapist listings on the internet. They are relatively inexpensive and increasing numbers of people use them. Also, get comfortable with couples work. In all the years I've been in private practice as a family therapist, a majority of the people coming to see me have been couples.*
> ~ Daniel Minuchin, MA, LMFT, AAMFT Approved Supervisor, Senior Faculty Member at the Minuchin Center for the Family, New York

- List your practice on social networking sites, such as:

  www.facebook.com
  www.myspace.com

- List your practice on sites local to your geographical area, such as:

  www.citysearch.com
  www.craigslist.com
  www.yelp.com

- Google Adwords: When you do a search online, you will notice a list of ads, also called "sponsored links," running down the far right side of your screen or along the top. You can create these mini-ads for your website so that when someone searches for a therapist in your area, s/he sees your ad. You only pay when someone clicks on your ad.

  Setting up a Google adwords campaign can be tricky. You can either read up on it yourself, or hire a professional.

  www.adwords.google.com

Formally Announce Your Practice

Mail or personally deliver a practice announcement package to all potential referral sources. This package will consist of a personalized note, a practice announcement, a few business cards (one for your referral source, and the others to hand out), and a couple of brochures.

See Appendix C for an example of a personalized note.

See Appendix D for an example of a practice announcement.

> TIP: SEND THIS PACKAGE TO ALL OF THE NETWORKING PROFESSIONALS YOU MET WHILE YOU WERE AN INTERN AND TO ANYONE ELSE YOU KNOW, PERSONALLY OR PROFESSIONALY, WHO MIGHT BE A REFERRAL SOURCE.

Since the cost of making and mailing a practice announcement package can add up quickly, target the best referral sources for your niche. A good referral source is someone who does business with your ideal client but is not a direct competitor. For example, if you want to specialize in working with young boys with ADHD, you might want to target local pediatricians, psychiatrists, mother's groups, and schools.

Consider the following list of referral sources, and choose which might be a good referral source for your niche:

- Doctors: general practitioners, pediatricians, oncologists, plastic surgeons, obstetricians, internists, dermatologists, etc.

- Lawyers

- Real estate agents

- Massage therapists

- Acupuncturists

- Corporate executives

- Mother's groups

- MFT training centers

- Alcohol and drug rehabilitation centers

- School administrators

- School counselors

- Psychiatrists

- Divorce mediators

- Hospice centers

- Life coaches

- Other: _____

- Other: _____

If you want or need referrals, let them know in your personalized note. It is common and acceptable to write: "I have a few spaces open in my practice that I am looking to fill," or "I would appreciate your thinking of me for referrals."

The best referral relationships go both ways, so write about how you can help them. Within two weeks of sending your packages, follow up with a short phone call.

> TIP: INVITE ONE POTENTIAL REFERRAL SOURCE TO COFFEE (AND PICK UP THE BILL) EACH WEEK.

Start a Newsletter

You can send out hard copies of a newsletter or take the easier and less expensive route of emailing your newsletter. If doing the latter, include a newsletter signup form on every page of your website to gather visitors' email addresses.

You can use one of the following resources to collect emails and to send out your newsletter via email en masse:

- www.iContact.com
- www.constantcontact.com
- www.aweber.com

> TIP: START SLOWLY, AND SEND OUT ONE NEWSLETTER EVERY THREE MONTHS.

If writing your own newsletter content seems overwhelming, hire someone else to do it from one of the following resources:

- www.warriorforum.com
- www.elance.com
- www.guru.com

Write Articles

Start getting known for your niche. Write an article (also called an "ezine") and publish it online on both your website and ezine marketing sites.

> TIP: RE-USE MATERIAL FROM YOUR NEWSLETTERS WHEN WRITING AN ARTICLE.

If writing your own articles seems over-whelming, hire someone to do it for you from one of the following resources:

- www.warriorforum.com
- www.elance.com
- www.guru.com

Where should you publish your articles online? Try one or more of these options:

- www.ezinearticles.com
- www.goarticles.com
- www.massivelinks.com

Sell Products on Your Website

While providing another form of revenue, selling products on your website also increases the likelihood that a buyer will return for more, i.e. contact you for therapy.

One option is to create customized CDs or DVDs to sell to potential customers. For example, if your niche is working with new mothers who have anxiety, record your own voice on a CD that teaches a few relaxation methods. Then sell these CDs, or give them away as promotional items.

Following are two resources to help you get started:

- www.thechillsessions.com
- www.audacity.sourceforge.net

Additional Marketing Resources

- Casey Truffo, MFT
  www.BeAWealthyTherapist.com
  www.BuildYourTherapyPractice.com

- Lynn Grodzki, LCSW
  www.PrivatePracticeSuccess.com

- Uncommon Practices
  www.uncommon-practices.com

- Annie Jennings PR
  www.anniejenningspr.com

Chapter 41
Networking

As mentioned earlier, networking is an integral part of building and maintaining a private practice. Although many therapists wait until they are licensed to begin networking, you will be ahead of the game if you start early.

A list of all resources mentioned in this chapter can be found in Appendix E.

Your Elevator Speech

Prepare your 30-second "elevator speech" that answers the inevitable question, "What do you do?" You will also deliver this sound bite anytime you introduce yourself to someone.

Learning to talk about what you do is often a challenge for both new and seasoned therapists. Many therapists report conversations coming to an abrupt halt when they mention their vocation.

While some people may be nervous about being psychoanalyzed when around a therapist, others may mistakenly believe that you possess mind-reading powers. Some may just not know what to say or ask.

Whatever biases you may encounter, you will benefit from learning how to speak confidently about your practice. This ability will put others at ease and will also increase your referrals.

As Lynn Grodzki teaches in her workbook called "Twelve Months To Your Ideal Private Practice," there are some basic message styles you can customize to make your elevator speech succinct and interesting.

Following are two templates of Lynn's suggested message styles:

1. "I specialize in _____. What I enjoy (value, appreciate, love) about my work is _____."

2. "If you _____, then I'm the kind of therapist who can help you to _____."

Try each style out below to see which feels more natural. Change it as needed to better suit your style. Make it yours!

TIP: WHENEVER YOU GO ANYWHERE (INCLUDING TO THE MARKET OR RUNNING A SIMPLE ERRAND), MAKE SURE YOU ARE ALWAYS ARMED WITH PLENTY OF BUSINESS CARDS. JOTTING DOWN A NOTE FOR SOMEONE? DO IT ON THE BACK OF YOUR BUSINESS CARD.

Professional Associations

Join the local chapters of your professional associations, if you have not already done so. These associations host monthly networking events, trainings, and speaking events.

Attend as many events as you possible, and mix and mingle. Bring plenty of business cards, and be sure to ask people for their business cards, too.

TIP: ALWAYS FOLLOW UP WITH NEW CONTACTS WITH A SHORT HANDWRITTEN NOTE OR EMAIL WITHIN A FEW DAYS. YOU ARE BUILDING YOUR REFERRAL NETWORK!

Network Online

It is also worthwhile to explore online networking sites. A couple of examples include:

www.LinkedIn.com
www.Jobster.com

Afterword

Thank you for reading this book. I hope these pages have given you a better sense of what the road to becoming a successful MFT entails and how best to get there.

You now have the tools you need to integrate with your education, training and experience to reach your goals of becoming a successful and licensed MFT. Are you ready?

Take a moment to think about any obstacles you may encounter on your MFT path. What can you do about them? What might these obstacles be telling you? Are there any particular topics discussed in this book that leave you with further questions? Did anything you read bring up feelings of doubt or anxiety? What's next for you?

If you would like additional support on your road to becoming a successful MFT where your specific questions and concerns can be addressed, I encourage you to contact me for a private consultation.

Remember, you can reach your MFT career goals, and you do not need to suffer along the way!

Appendix A
Sample Thank You Letters

Example One

Your Full Name
Your Full Address
Your Phone Number

Their Full Name
Name of School
Their Full Address
Date

Dear [Ms. Lemmein],

It was a pleasure meeting you yesterday during the interview process for [Name of school]'s MFT program. I really enjoyed our conversation about [the growing trends in the field, and I look forward to reading the book you recommended].

Thank you again for your time, and I hope to see you in the fall!

Sincerely,

Your Signature

Your Printed Full Name

Example Two

Your Full Name
Your Full Address
Your Phone Number

Their Full Name
Name of School
Their Full Address
Date

Dear [Dr. Axseptme],

I greatly enjoyed meeting you today while interviewing for your MFT program. [Name of school] remains my top choice, and I was very impressed by [the training facilities and available fieldwork resources.]

I feel your program is a perfect match for me and look forward to contributing to your long line of successful graduates!

Sincerely,

Your Signature

Your Printed Full Name

Appendix B
Sample Practice Niches

Populations	Problems
Animal lovers	Pet loss
Artists	Fearful of success
Teachers	Job dissatisfaction
Single mothers	Chronic illness
Toddlers	ADHD
Engaged couples	Communication skills
Lawyers	Chemical dependency
Divorced fathers	Money issues
Retirees	Depression
College students	Anxiety
LGBT	Self-esteem issues
Step-parents	Parenting issues
Mothers of the bride	Relationship issues with bride
Couples	Infertility
Recently widowed	Bereavement
CEOs	Lack of relationship
New parents	Parenting skills
Single women	Negative dating patterns
Nice guys	Can't say no
Teenagers	Self-destructive behavior
Females	Unhappy marriage
Parents of twins	Time management issues
Divorced couples	Co-parenting issues
Empty nesters	Adjustment problems
Professional athletes	Relationship problem
New mothers	Post-partum depression
Disabled	Sexual issues
Elderly	Pain management

Appendix C
Sample Personalized Note

Handwritten On Your Letterhead

[Date]

Dear [Dr. Enfant],

As an infertility specialist, you see many patients struggle with the difficult cycle of hope, anxiety, and depression around trying to conceive. As a psychotherapist in private practice, I specialize in working with couples who are struggling with fertility issues. I would like to extend my services to your patients and think we could be great mutual referral sources for each other.

I have enclosed some materials about my practice for your review, including a brochure about an infertility group for couples that I am currently forming. I have spaces available in this group and would appreciate your keeping me in mind for referrals.

I will call you next week to discuss how I might be of service to you and your patients and look forward to speaking with you then.

Best,

Your Signature (sign legibly)

Appendix D
Sample Practice Announcement

CRIS WALKER ROSKELLEY

Licensed Marriage and Family Therapist

is pleased to announce
the opening of her psychotherapy practice:

Growing Through Transition · Mastering Change

**Services include child, adolescent, adult,
couples, and group therapy**

Examples of life transitions include:
Starting kindergarten · Developmental milestones
Introducing a new sibling · Puberty · Graduations
Leaving for college · Getting married · Career changes
Moving · Becoming a parent · Divorce · Injury
Empty nest · Retirement · Loss of a loved one

— • • • —

350 Bon Air Rd. · Suite 140
Greenbrae · CA · 94904
T: 415 · 289 · 2111
E: cris@MarinCountyCounseling.com
W: www.MarinCountyCounseling.com

Day and Evening Appointments Available
Your referrals are welcome and appreciated

Appendix E
Resource Listings

AAMFT

- www.aamft.org

Blogs

- www.mfthandbook.blogspot.com
- www.mftinterns.wordpress.com
- www.mftsfbay.blogspot.com

Business Plan

- www.sba.gov/smallbusinessplanner/index.html

California

- www.bbs.ca.gov
- www.bbs.ca.gov/bd_activity/mft_educ_comm_update.shtml
- www.bbs.ca.gov/app-reg/exp_calc.shtml
- www.camft.org

Credit Cards

- www.propay.com
- www.professionalcharges.com
- www.paypal.com

Exam Study Materials

- www.gerrygrossman.com
- www.aatbs.com
- www.passmftexams.com

Google Marketing

- www.adwords.google.com

Graphic Design

- www.99designs.com
- www.elogocontest.com
- www.gfxcontest.com
- www.guru.com
- www.elance.com
- www.warriorforum.com

Hours Tracking

- www.TrackYourHours.com
- www.Arsene.com

Imprinter

- www.portaprint.com

Internship/Job Searches

- www.craigslist.com
- www.alltherapyjobs.com
- www.socialservice.com
- www.jobster.com

Maps

- www.maps.google.com
- www.mapquest.com

Marketing Professionals

- www.beawealthytherapist.com
- www.privatepracticesuccess.com
- www.uncommon-practices.com
- www.anniejenningspr.com

Networking

- www.facebook.com
- www.myspace.com
- www.linkedin.com
- www.jobster.com

Newsletters, Articles, and Autoresponders

- www.iContact.com
- www.constantcontact.com
- www.aweber.com
- www.ezinearticles.com
- www.goarticles.com
- www.massivelinks.com
- www.warriorforum.com

Office Search

- www.craigslist.com
- www.psychoffice.net

Online Directories

- www.find-a-therapist.com
- www.goodtherapy.org
- www.psychologytoday.com

- www.counsel-search.com
- www.networktherapy.com
- www.theramatch.com
- www.yellowpages.com
- www.4therapy.com
- www.insiderpages.com
- www.wellness.com
- www.everytherapist.com
- www.counselingbook.com
- www.citysearch.com
- www.craigslist.com
- www.yelp.com
- www.facebook.com
- www.myspace.com

Practice Management

- www.quickbooks.com
- www.argonautsoftware.com
- www.helper.com
- www.notes444.com
- www.quicdoc.com
- www.practicemagic.com

Professional Associations

- www.camft.org
- www.sandplay.org
- www.arttherapy.org
- www.aplb.org
- www.a4pt.org
- www.nadt.org
- www.aabt.org

- www.adta.org
- www.ieata.org
- www.musictherapy.org
- www.tdi-dog.org
- www.ahta.org
- www.apmha.com
- www.ifta-familytherapy.org
- www.agpa.org

Recordings

- www.thechillsessions.com
- www.audacity.sourceforge.net

Stationary

- www.99designs.com
- www.vistaprint.com
- www.overnightprints.com
- www.printplace.com

Taxes

- www.turbotax.com
- www.irs.gov/business/small

Websites

- www.fortherapists.com
- www.webpowertools.com
- www.therapistwebsites.com
- www.therapysites.com
- www.homestead.com
- www.godaddy.com

Appendix F
Recommended Reading

The Profession

- Yalom, Irvin. (2002). *The Gift of Therapy.* New York: Harper Perennial.

- Pipher, Mary. (2003). *Letters To A Young Therapist.* New York: Basic Books.

- Kottler, Jeffrey. (2003). *On Being A Therapist.* San Francisco: Jossey-Bass.

- Bender, Suzanne & Messner, Edward. (2003). *Becoming A Therapist.* New York: Guilford Press.

- Rabinowitz, Ilana. (1998). *Inside Therapy.* New York: St. Martin's Press.

Marketing

- Truffo, Casey. (2007). *Be a Wealthy Therapist: Finally You Can Make A Living While Making A Difference.* Saint Peters, CA: MP Press.

- Grodzki, Lynn. (2003). *Twelve Months to Your Ideal Private Practice: A Workbook.* New York: Norton.

- Grand, Laurie Cope. (2000). *The Marriage and Family Presentation Guide.* New York: Wiley.

- Grand, Laurie Cope. (2002). *The Therapist's Advertising and Marketing Kit*. New York: Wiley.

- Grand, Laurie Cope. (2002). *The Therapist's Newsletter Kit*. New York: Wiley.

- Ruben, Douglas. (1997). *Writing for Money in Mental Health*. New York: Haworth Press.

- Kase, Larina. (2005). *The Successful Therapist*. New York: Wiley.

- Practice Management

- Zuckerman, Edward. (2003). *The Paper Office*. New York: Guilford Press.

- Wiger, Donald. (2005). *The Clinical Documentation Sourcebook*. New York: Wiley.

Index

About the Author

 **Cris Walker Roskelley** is a Licensed Marriage and Family Therapist whose goal is to demystify the process of becoming a successful MFT from graduate school through licensure... and beyond!

Cris regularly consults with aspiring MFTs on the licensing process and with newly licensed MFTs on setting up a successful practice. She also offers a complete design solution for MFTs in private practice including website, stationary and office design consultation services.

Specializing in helping people through major life transitions (like getting licensed!), Cris maintains a private practice in the San Francisco Bay Area.

Cris received her Master of Science degree in Counseling Psychology with a specialization in Marriage and Family Therapy from Dominican University of California. She received her Bachelor of Arts degree from Dartmouth College.

Cris has worked therapeutically with adults, children, adolescents, couples, families, and groups since 1992. As a consultant and keynote speaker, she educates and assists schools,

students, and organizations on the transition process.

Cris is also a Certified Prepare/Enrich Relationship Counselor and has had extensive training in the Gottman Method of Couples Therapy and Imago Relationship Therapy. She was selected to attend and speak at a United Nations Conference on Children's Rights in Geneva, Switzerland.

You are welcome to get in touch with Cris:

- To schedule a private consultation
- To inquire about design services
- To provide feedback
- To learn about upcoming book titles
- To inquire about joint ventures

By website: www.MFTHandbook.com
By email: cris@MFTHandbook.com

Quick Order Form

Email order: Publisher@FemmeOsagePublishing.com
Telephone order: (636) 922-2634
Fax order: (636) 410-6430

☐ **I wish to purchase the following book:**
_____ **(Quantity)**
"On the Road To Becoming a Successful Marriage and Family Therapist: An Insider's Handbook from Graduate School Through Licensure... and Beyond!"

Please send me FREE information from Cris on:
☐ Future book titles ☐ Design Services
☐ Marketing Tips ☐ Consulting

All Fields Required:

Name: _____

Address: _____

City: _____ State: _____ Zip: _____

Telephone: _____

Email: _____

Missouri residents: Add 7.5% sales tax to your order.
Shipping: $6.00 for each book via USPS Media Mail.

Quick Order Form

Email order: Publisher@FemmeOsagePublishing.com
Telephone order: (636) 922-2634
Fax order: (636) 410-6430

☐ **I wish to purchase the following book:**
_____ **(Quantity)**
"On the Road To Becoming a Successful Marriage and Family Therapist: An Insider's Handbook from Graduate School Through Licensure... and Beyond!"

Please send me FREE information from Cris on:
☐ Future book titles ☐ Design Services
☐ Marketing Tips ☐ Consulting

All Fields Required:

Name: _____

Address: _____

City: _____ State: _____ Zip: _____

Telephone: _____

Email: _____

Missouri residents: Add 7.5% sales tax to your order.
Shipping: $6.00 for each book via USPS Media Mail.

See www.MFTHandbook.com/Links.html for more exclusive discounts!